I0485744

Coloring Books For Adults Vol. 2

40 Stress Relieving And Relaxing Patterns

Adult Coloring Books Series By
www.ColoringCraze.com

Copyright © 2019 ColoringCraze

All rights reserved.

ISBN: 1517049482

ISBN-13: 978-1517049485

Edition: 4

FREE GIFT FOR YOU!

Coloring books enthusiast? Get **Free Bonus Kit** from the site below:

=> http://www.coloringcraze.com/**bonus** <=

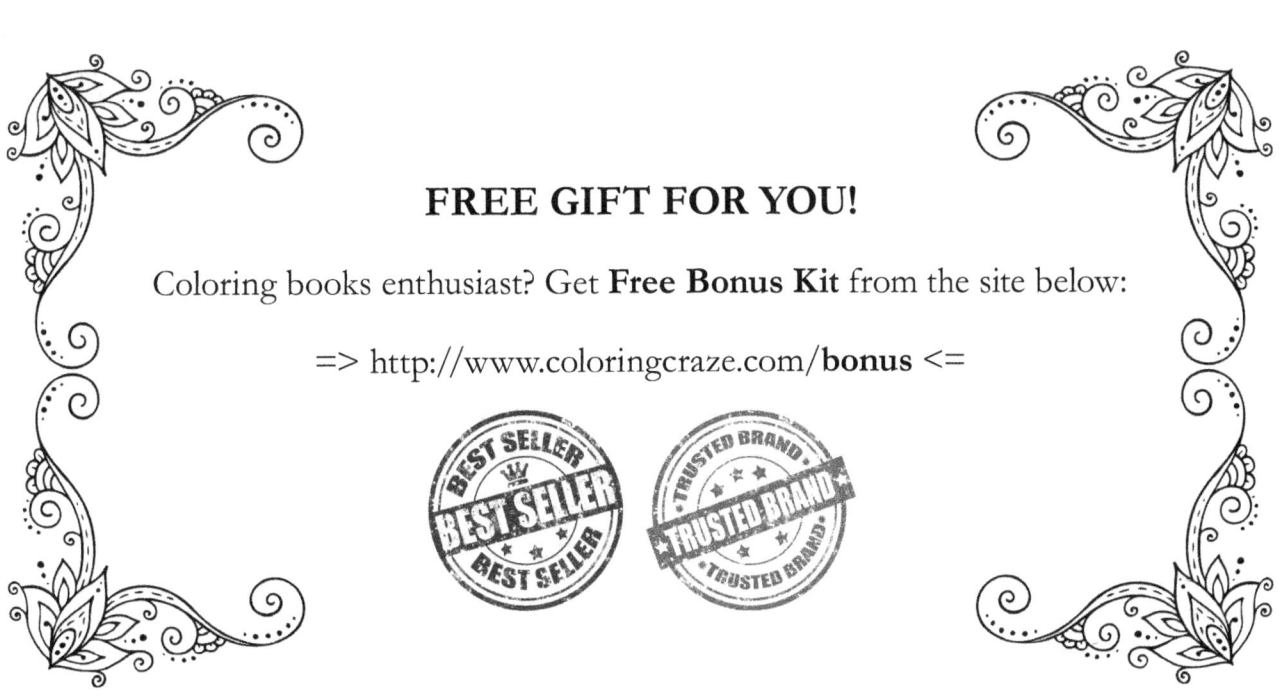

Test Your Colors Here

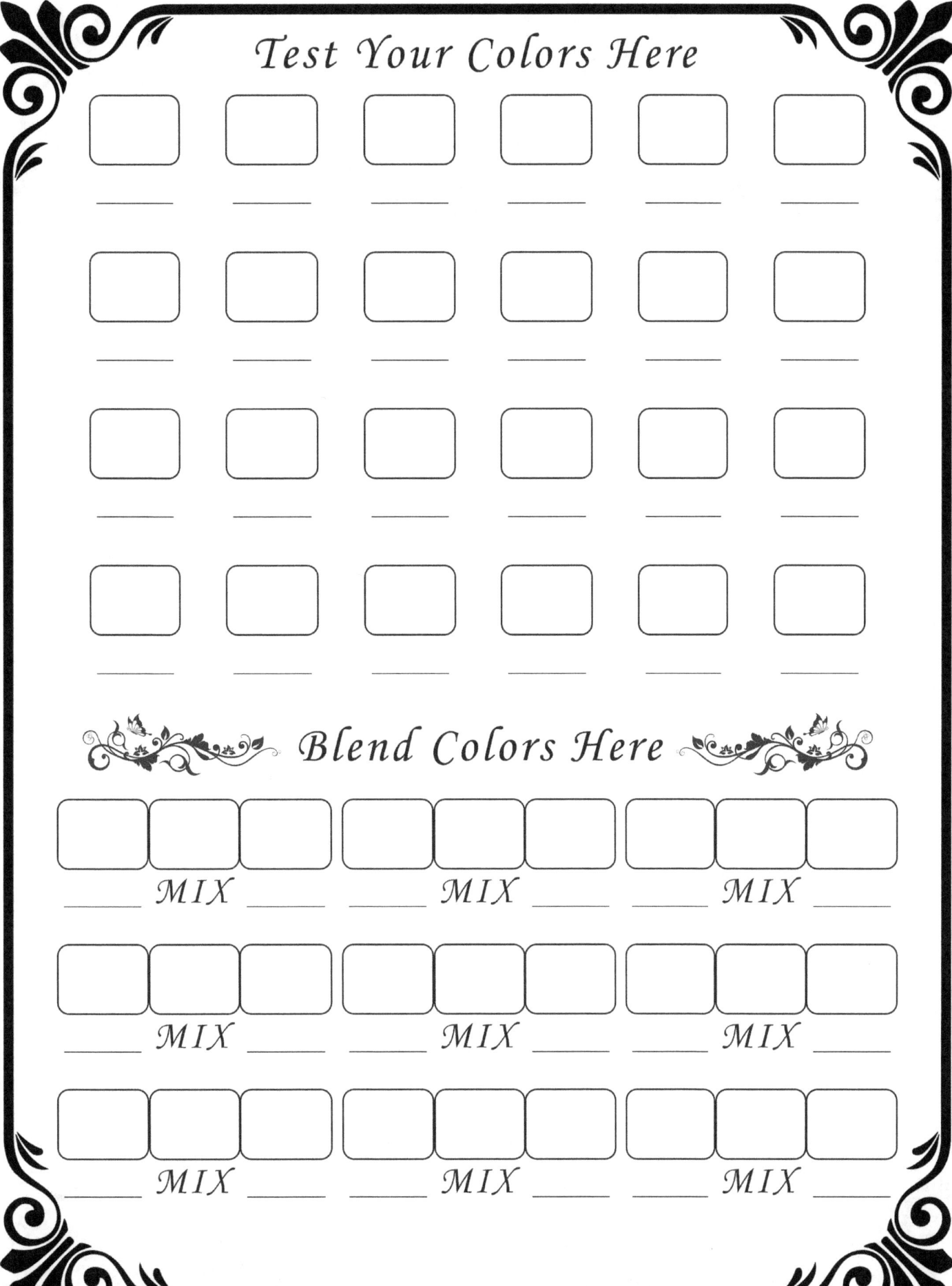

Blend Colors Here

___ ___ MIX ___ ___   ___ ___ MIX ___ ___   ___ ___ MIX ___ ___

___ ___ MIX ___ ___   ___ ___ MIX ___ ___   ___ ___ MIX ___ ___

___ ___ MIX ___ ___   ___ ___ MIX ___ ___   ___ ___ MIX ___ ___

Test Your Colors Here

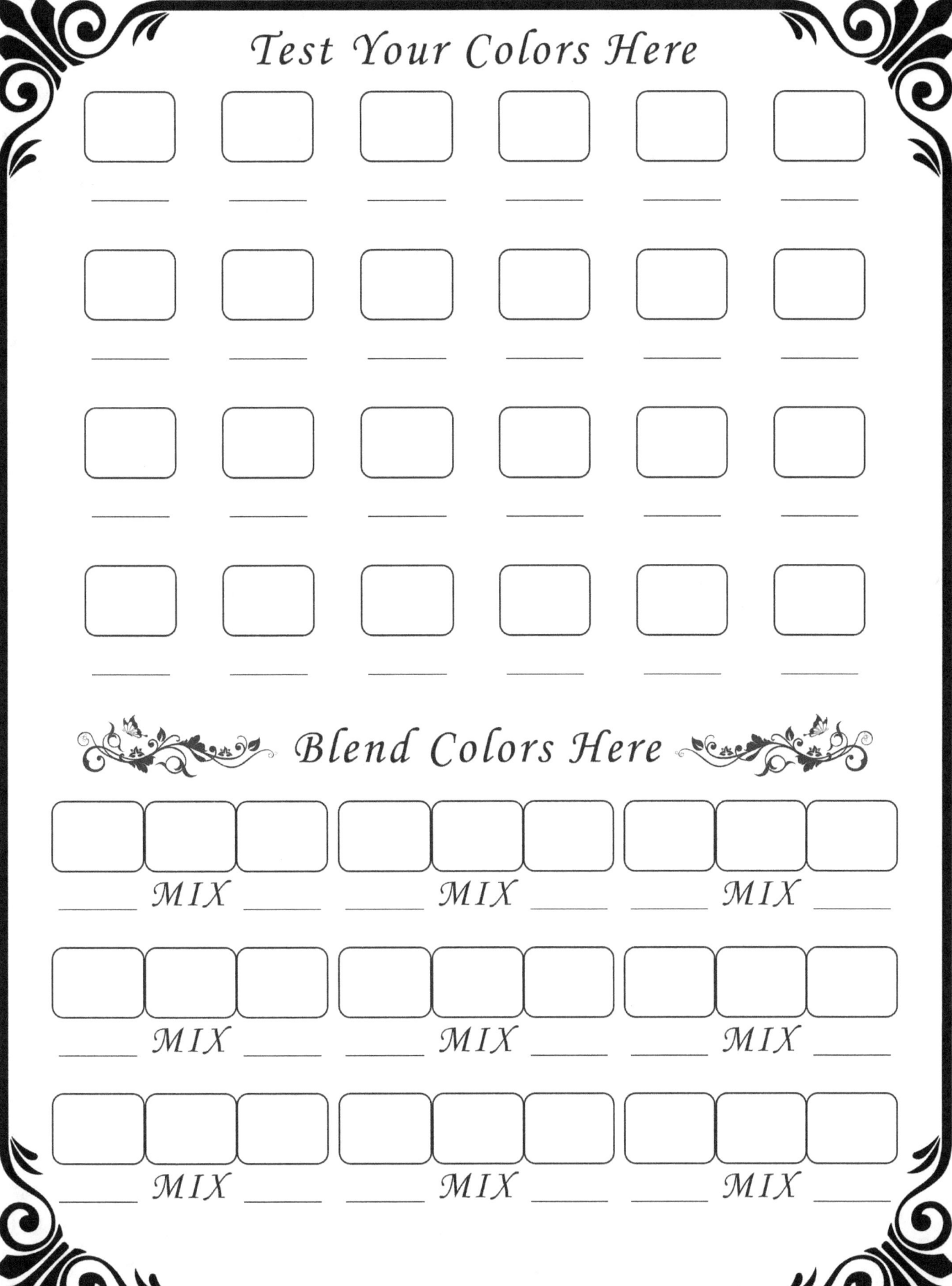

Blend Colors Here

MIX   MIX   MIX

MIX   MIX   MIX

MIX   MIX   MIX

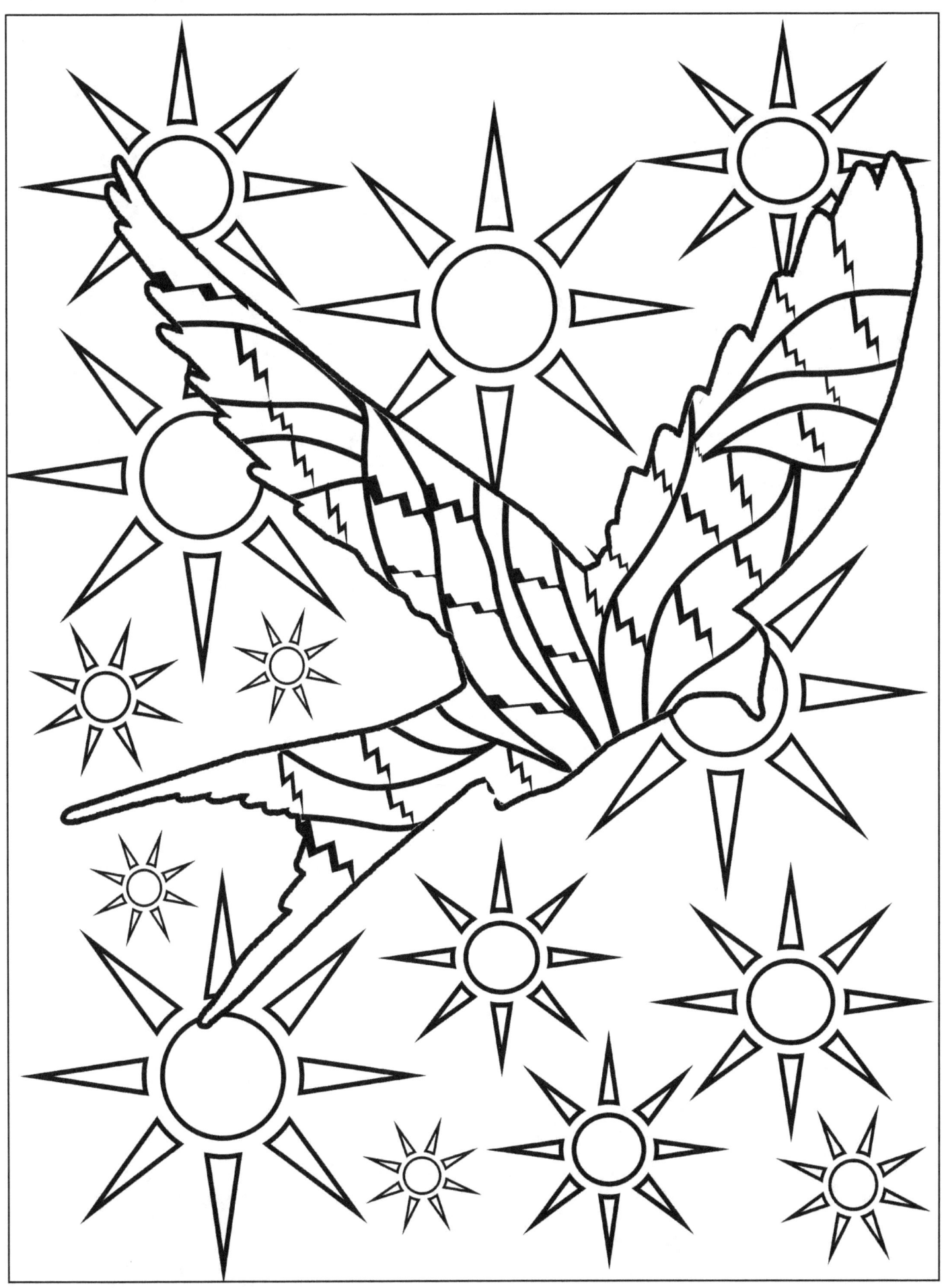

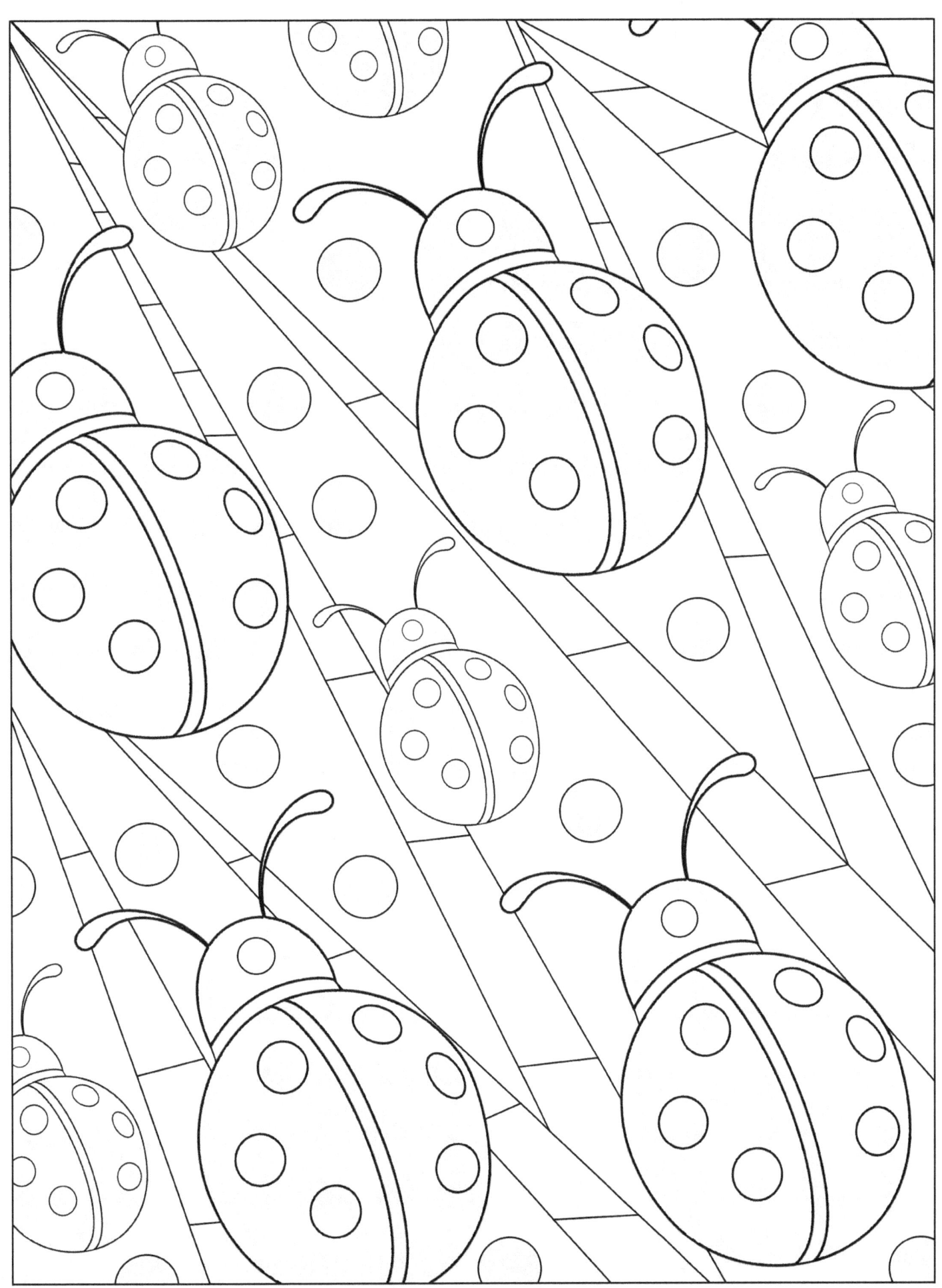

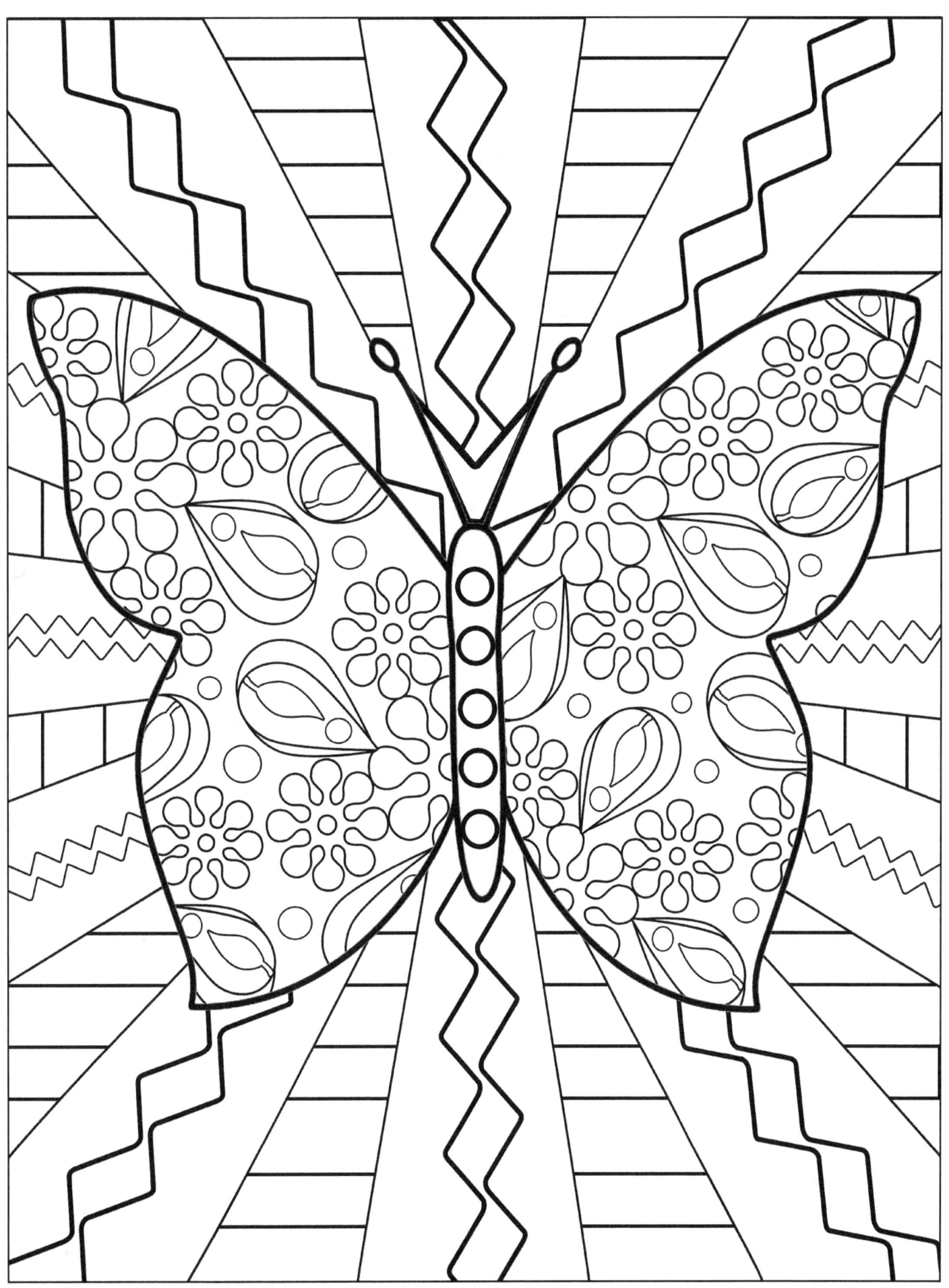

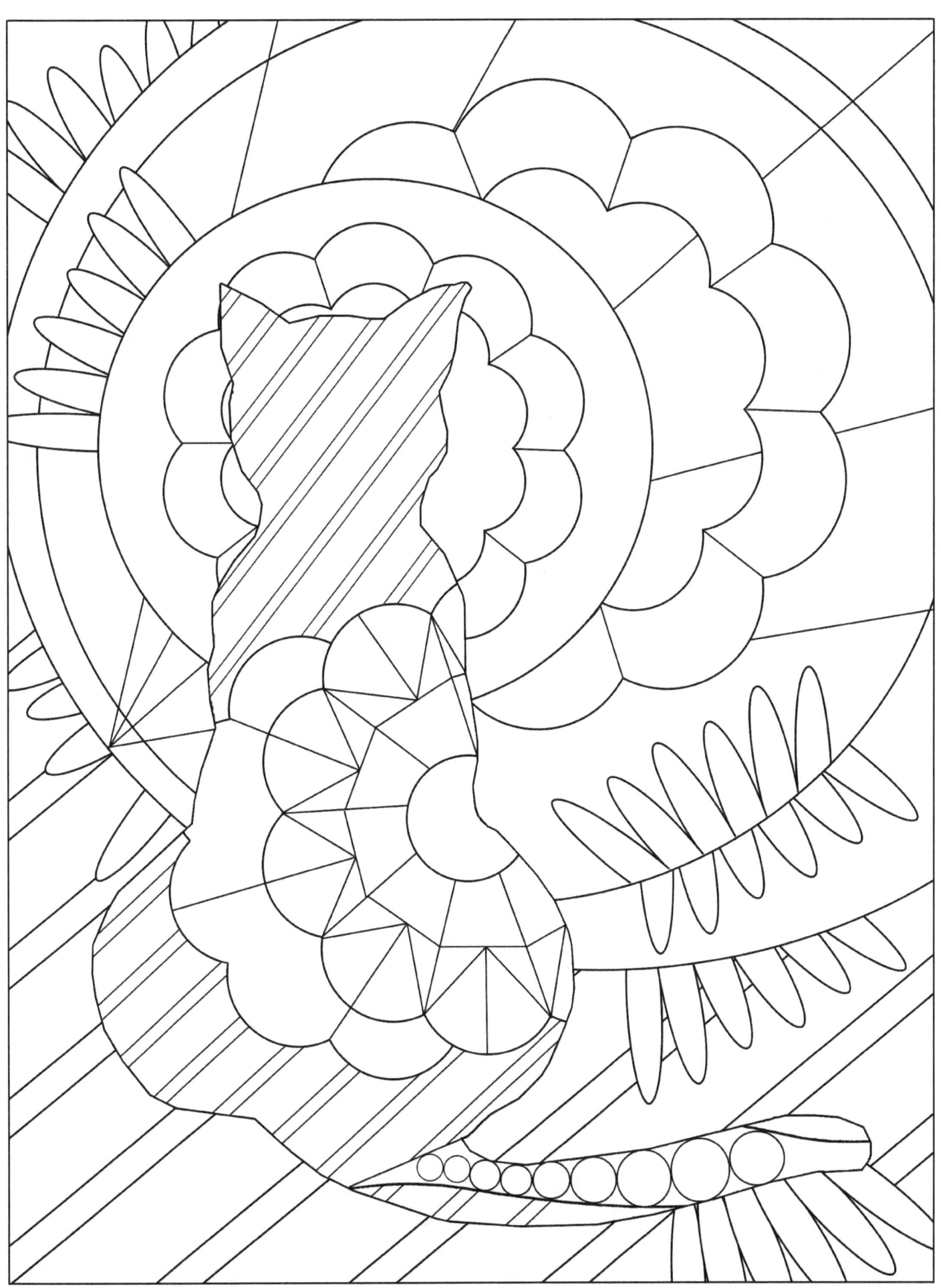

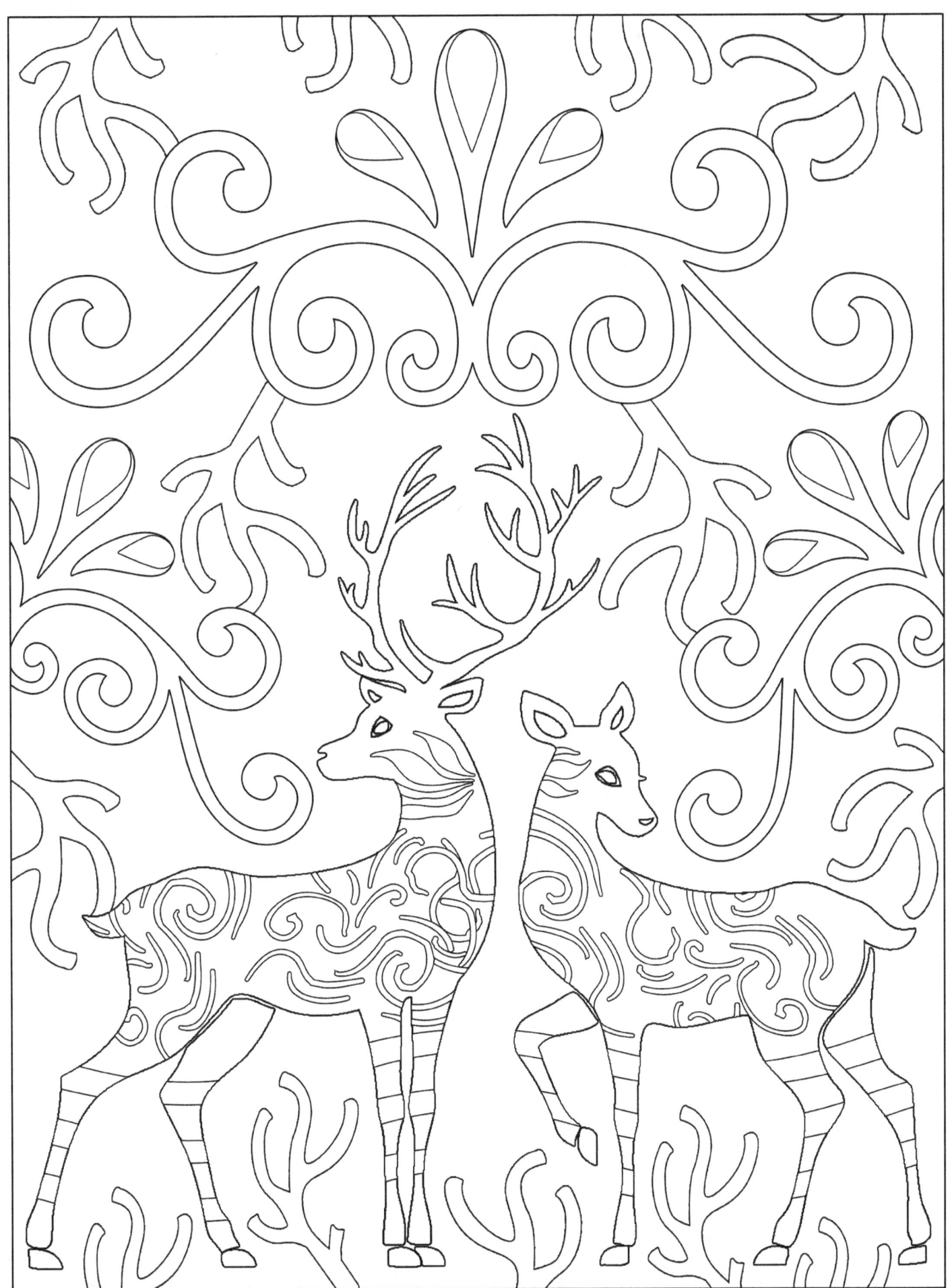

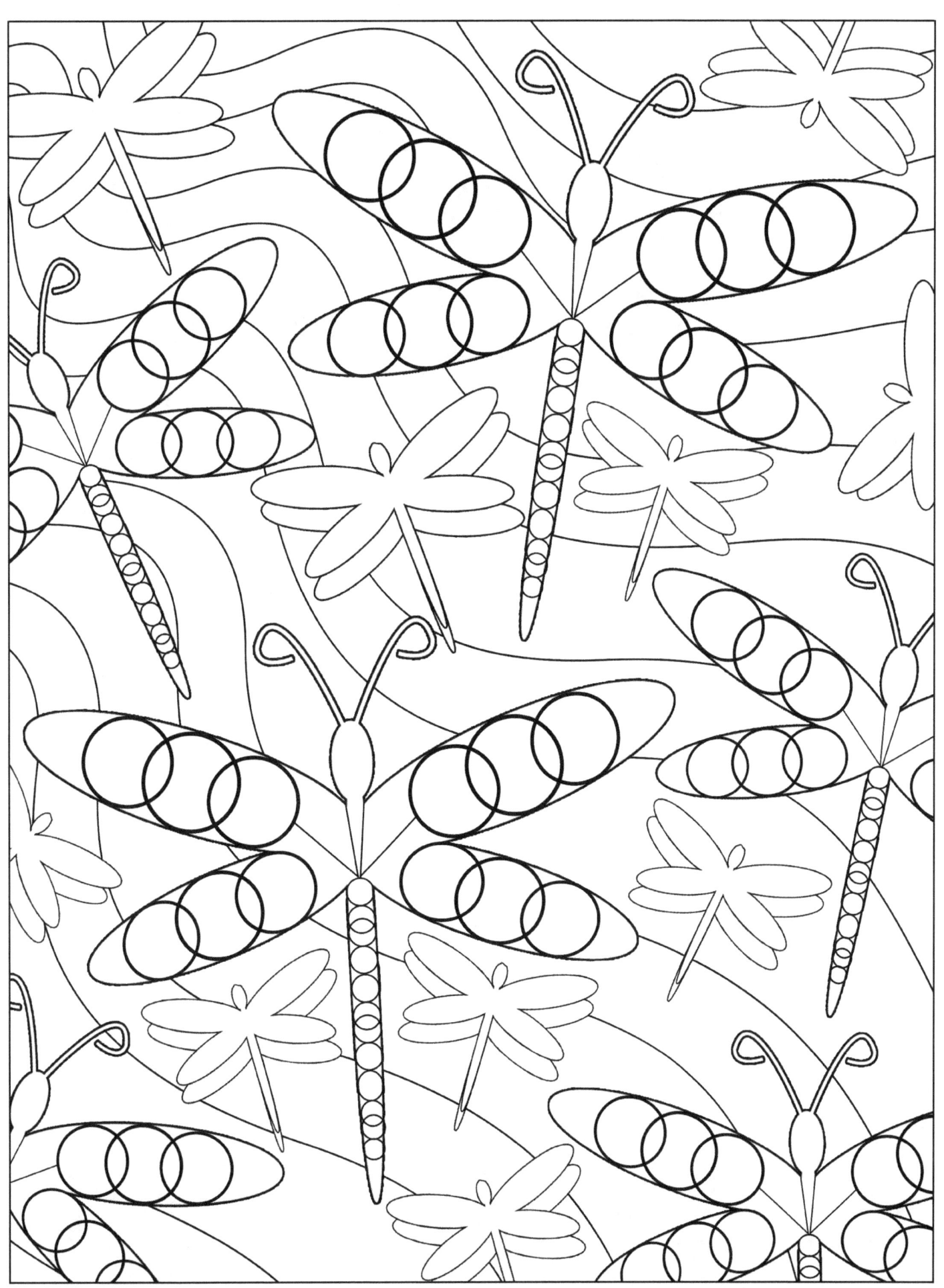

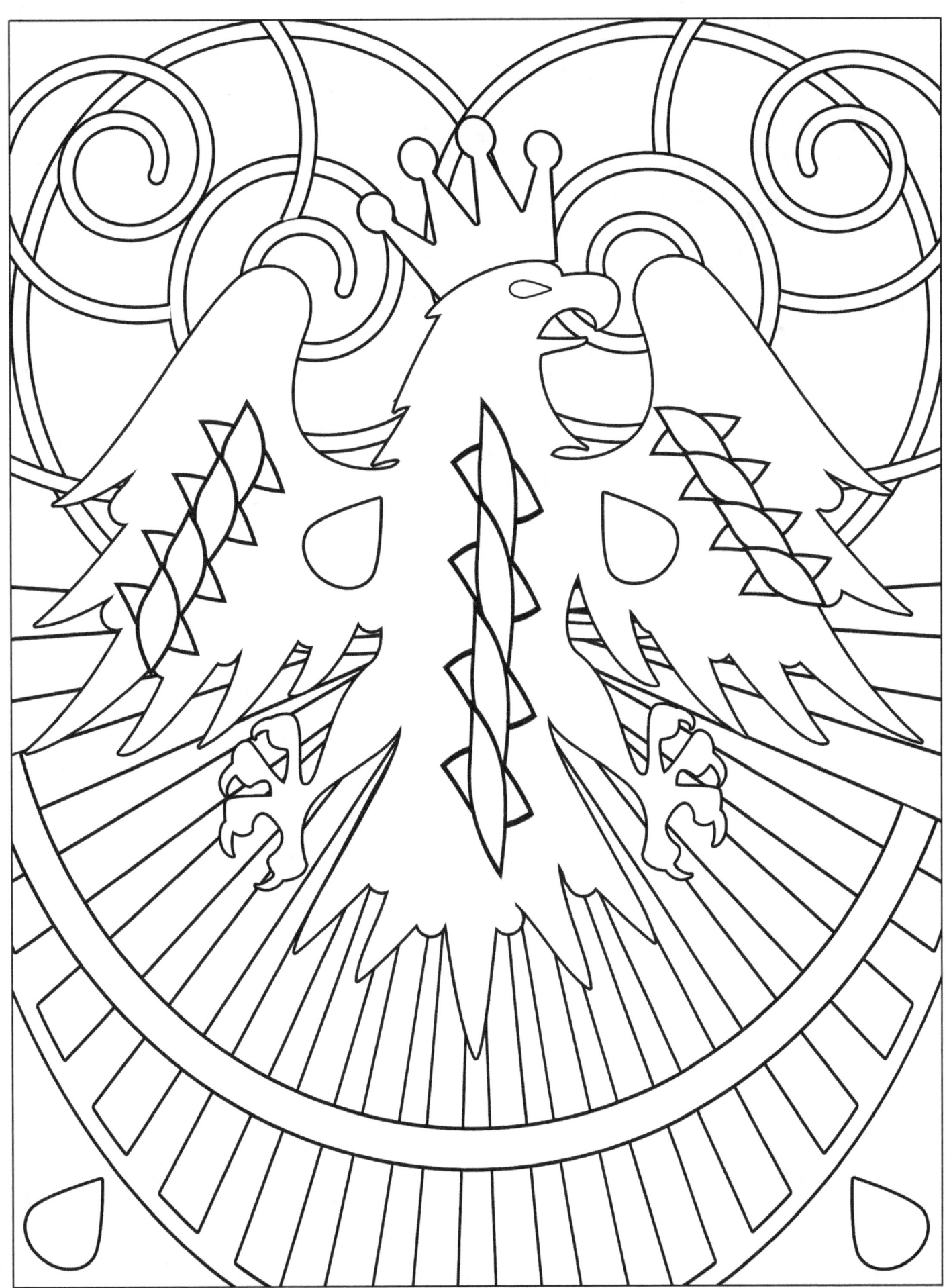

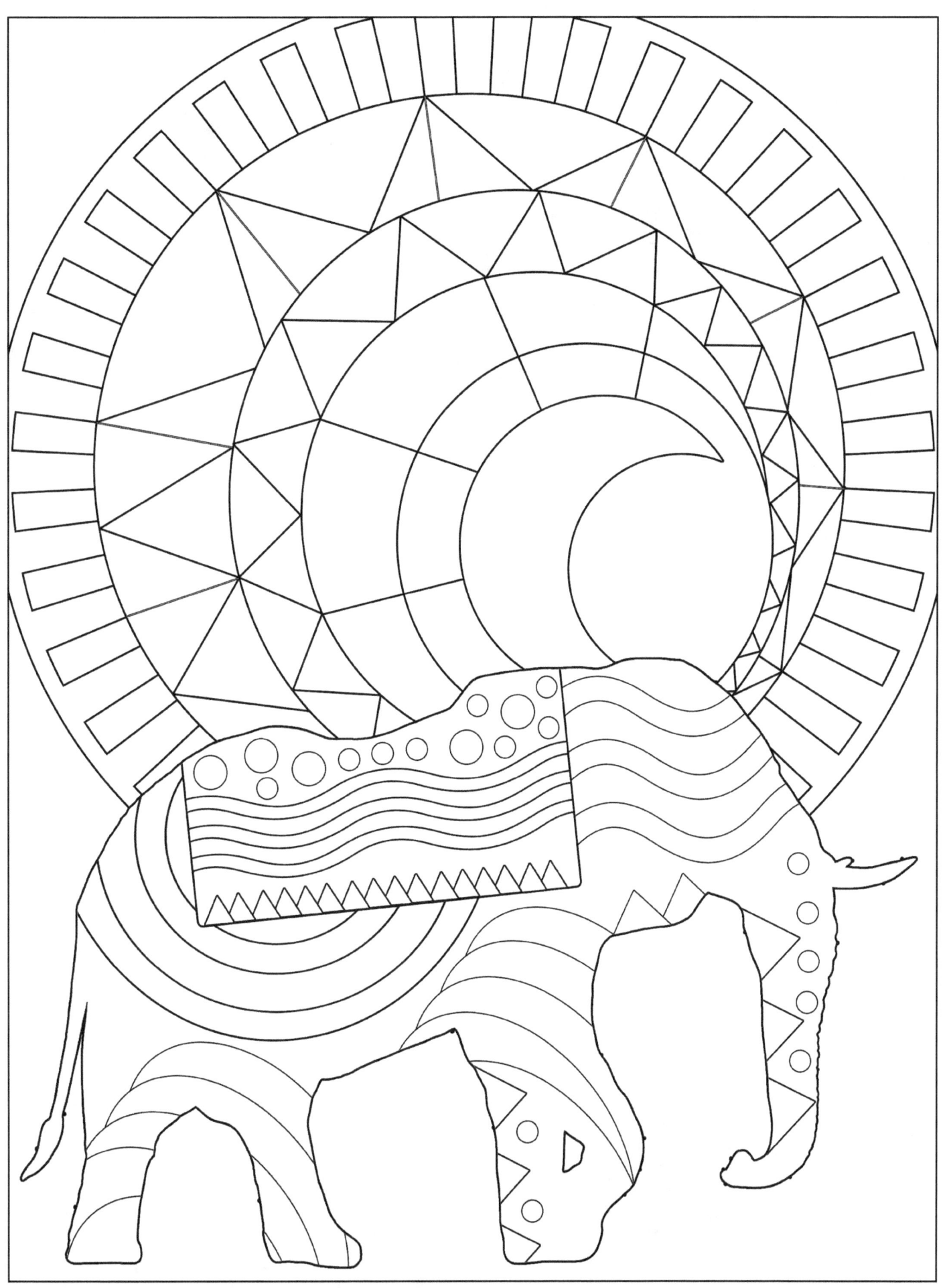

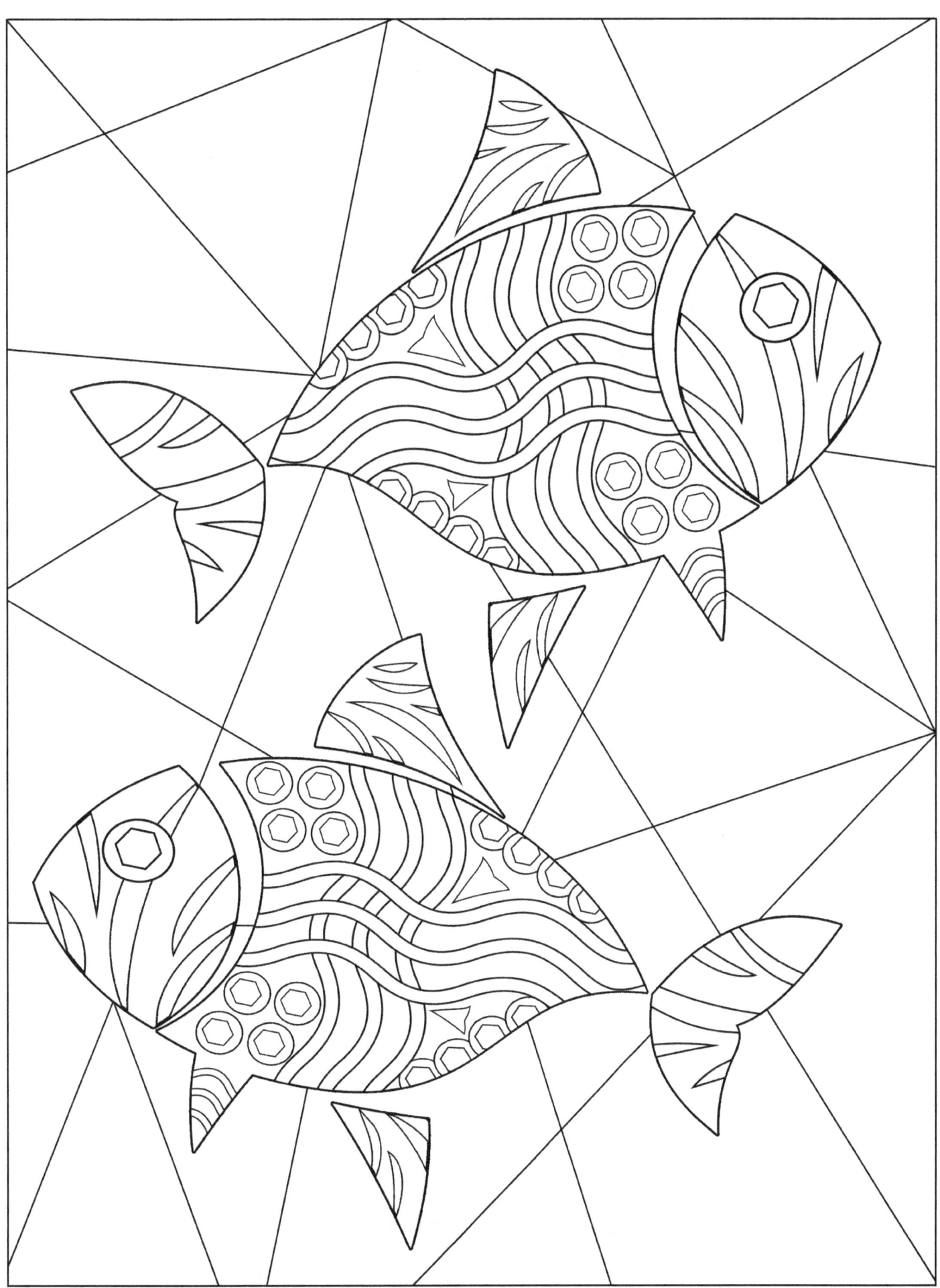

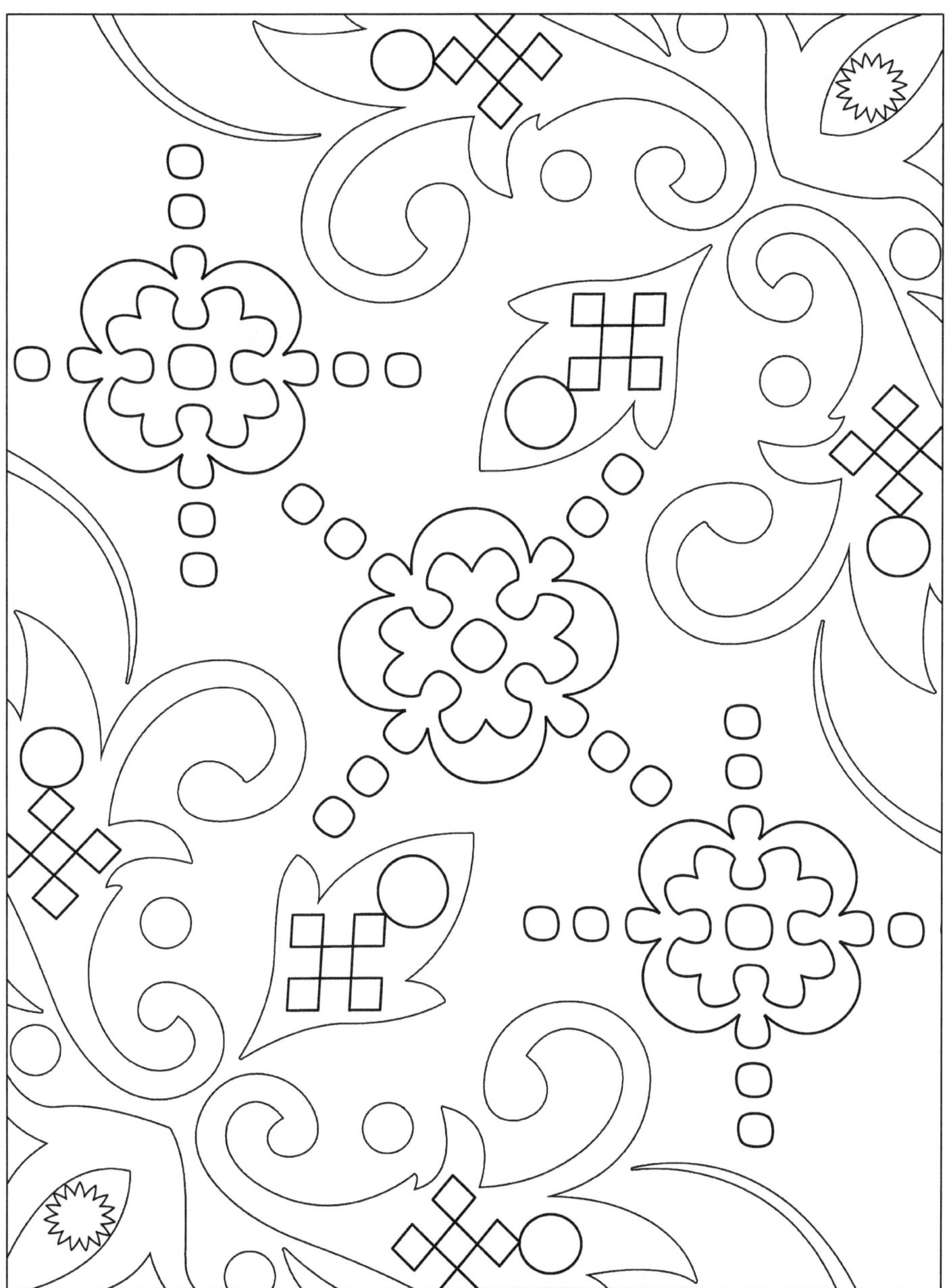

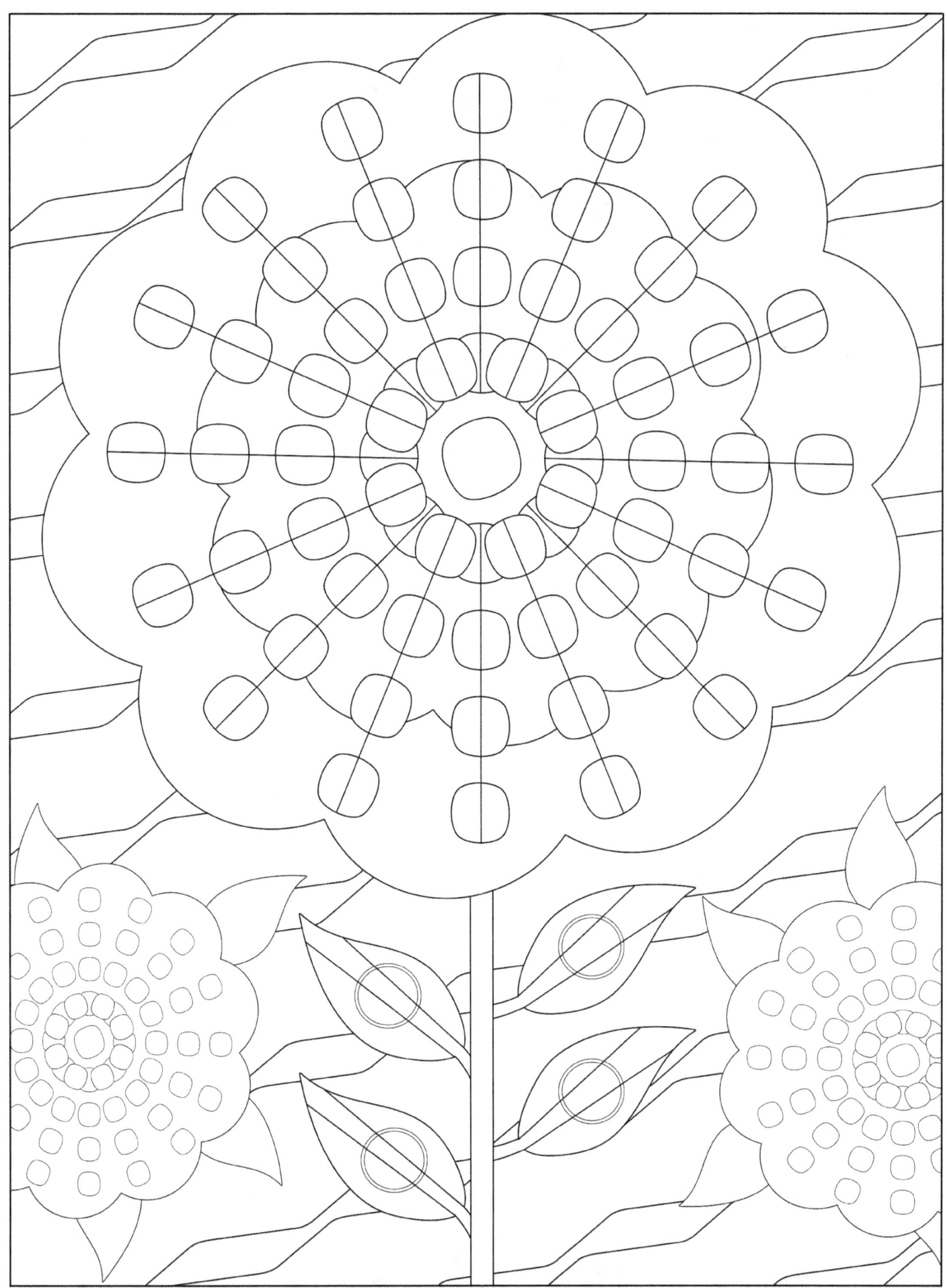

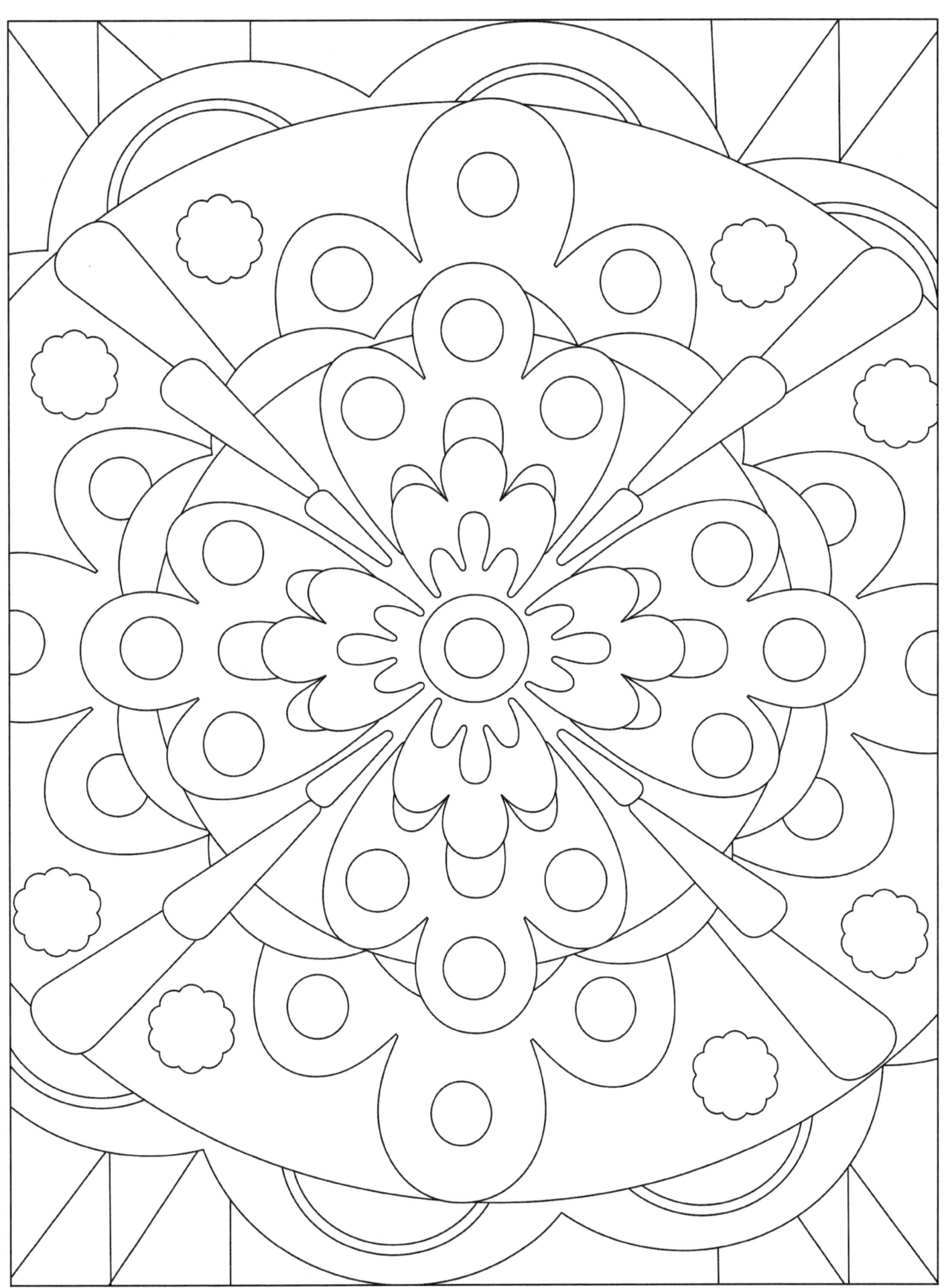

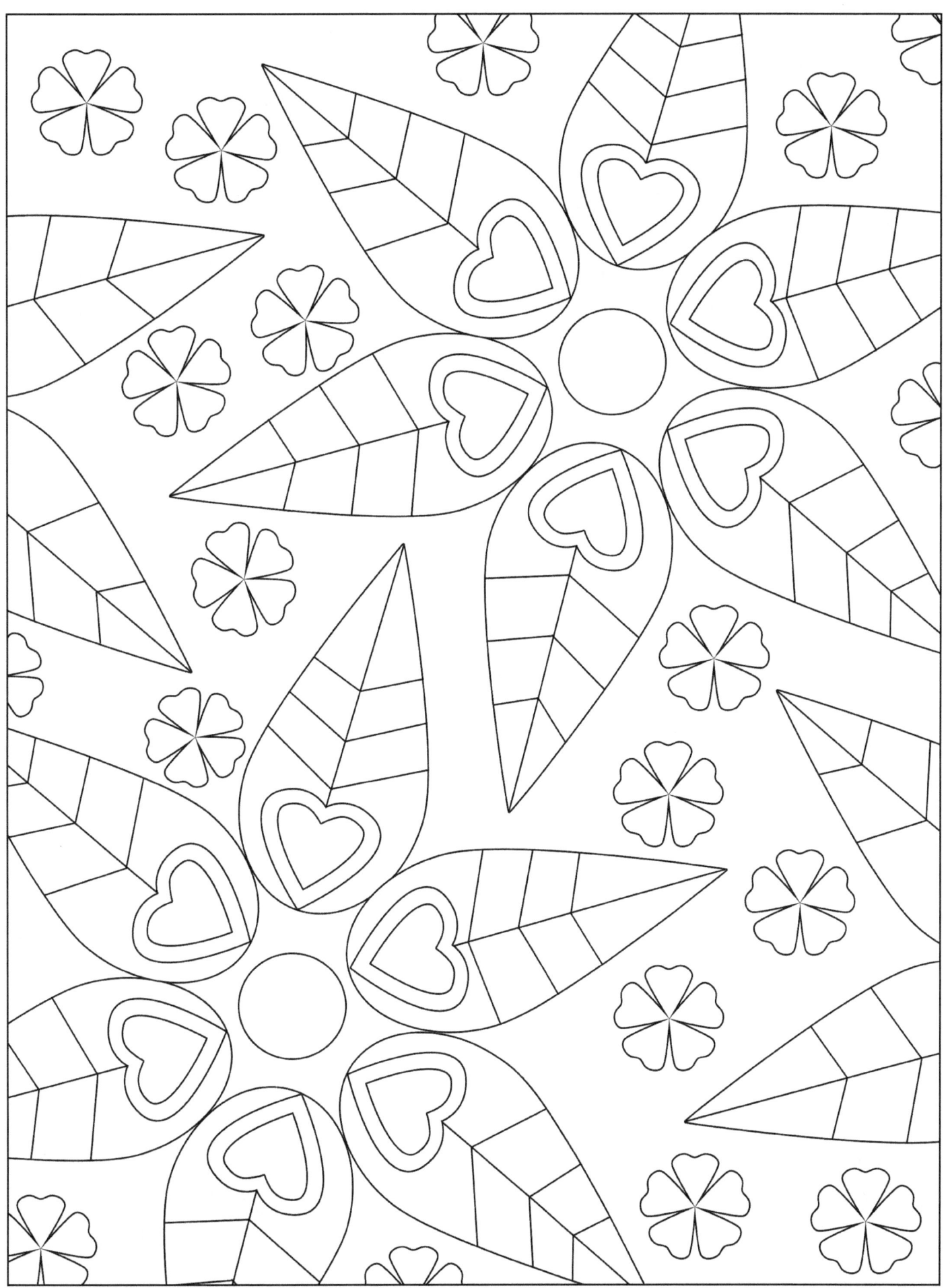

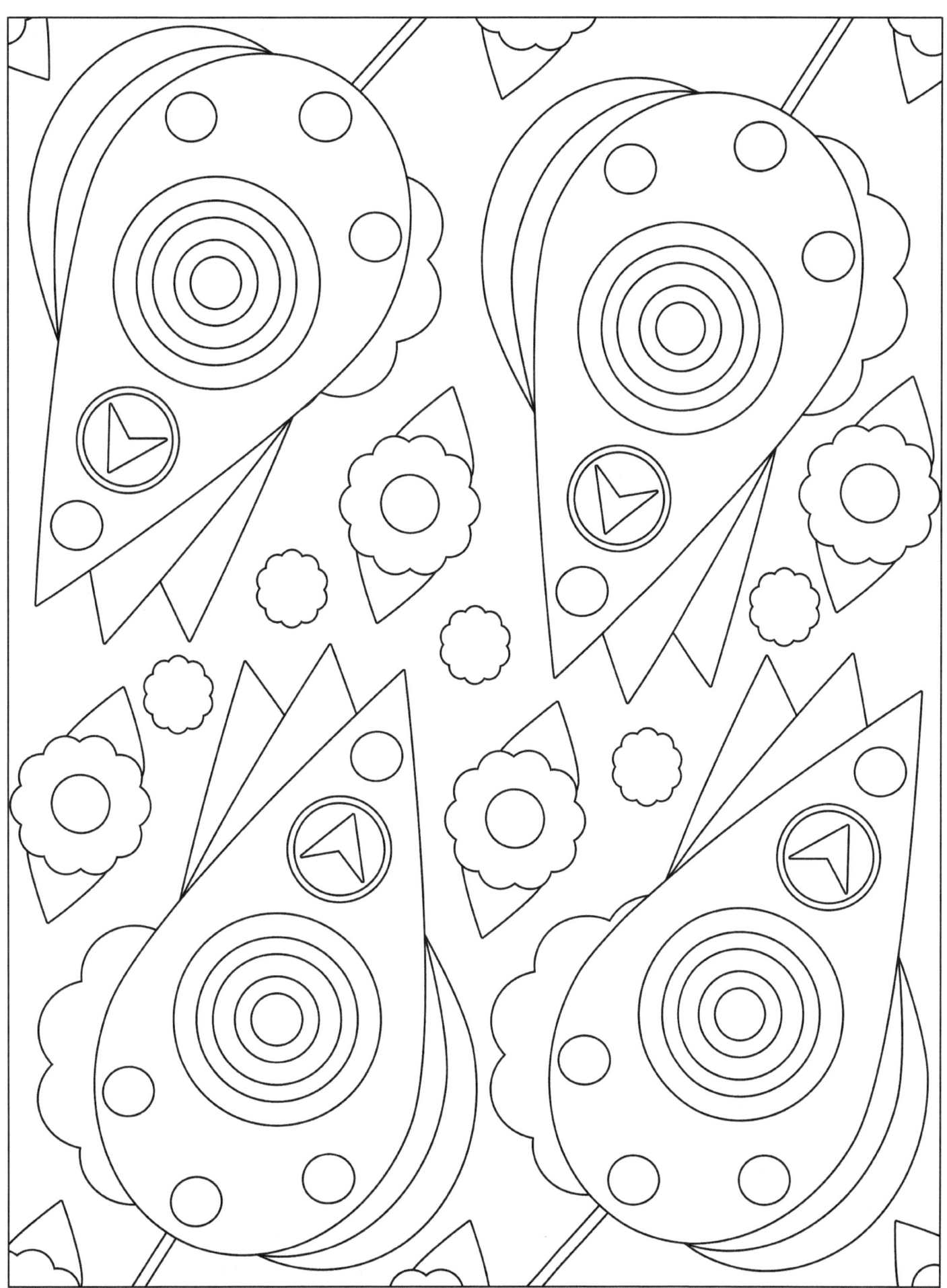

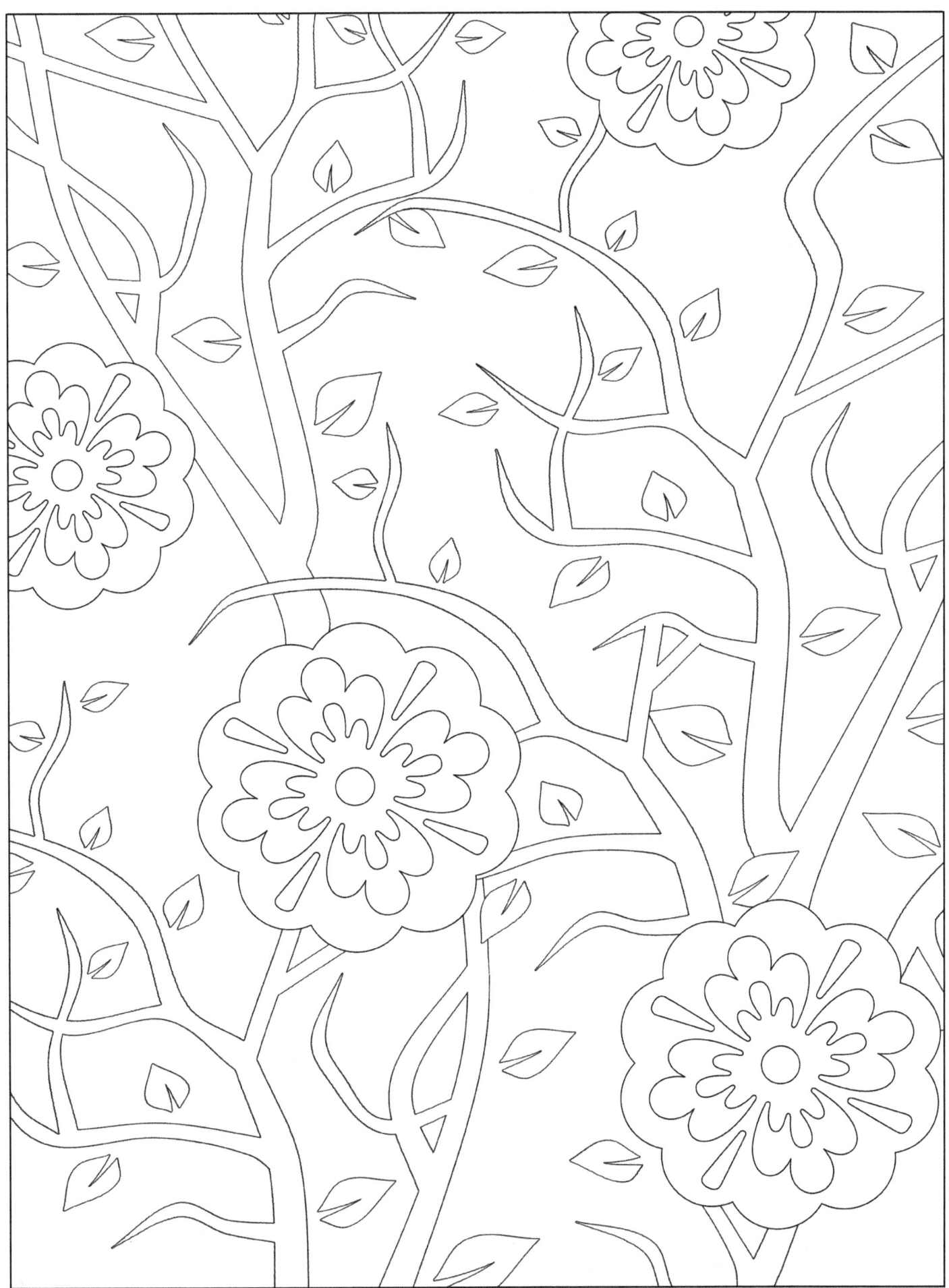

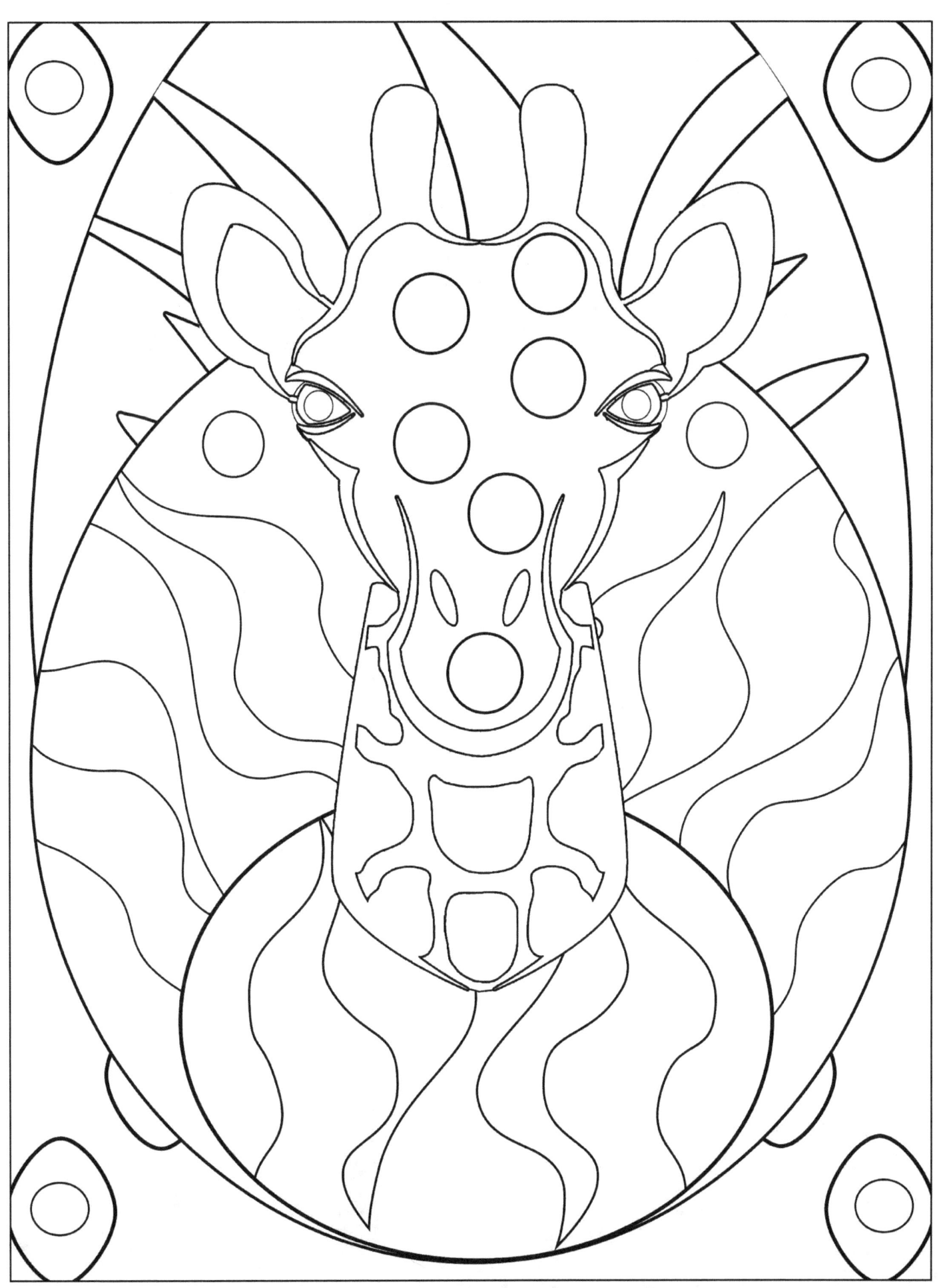

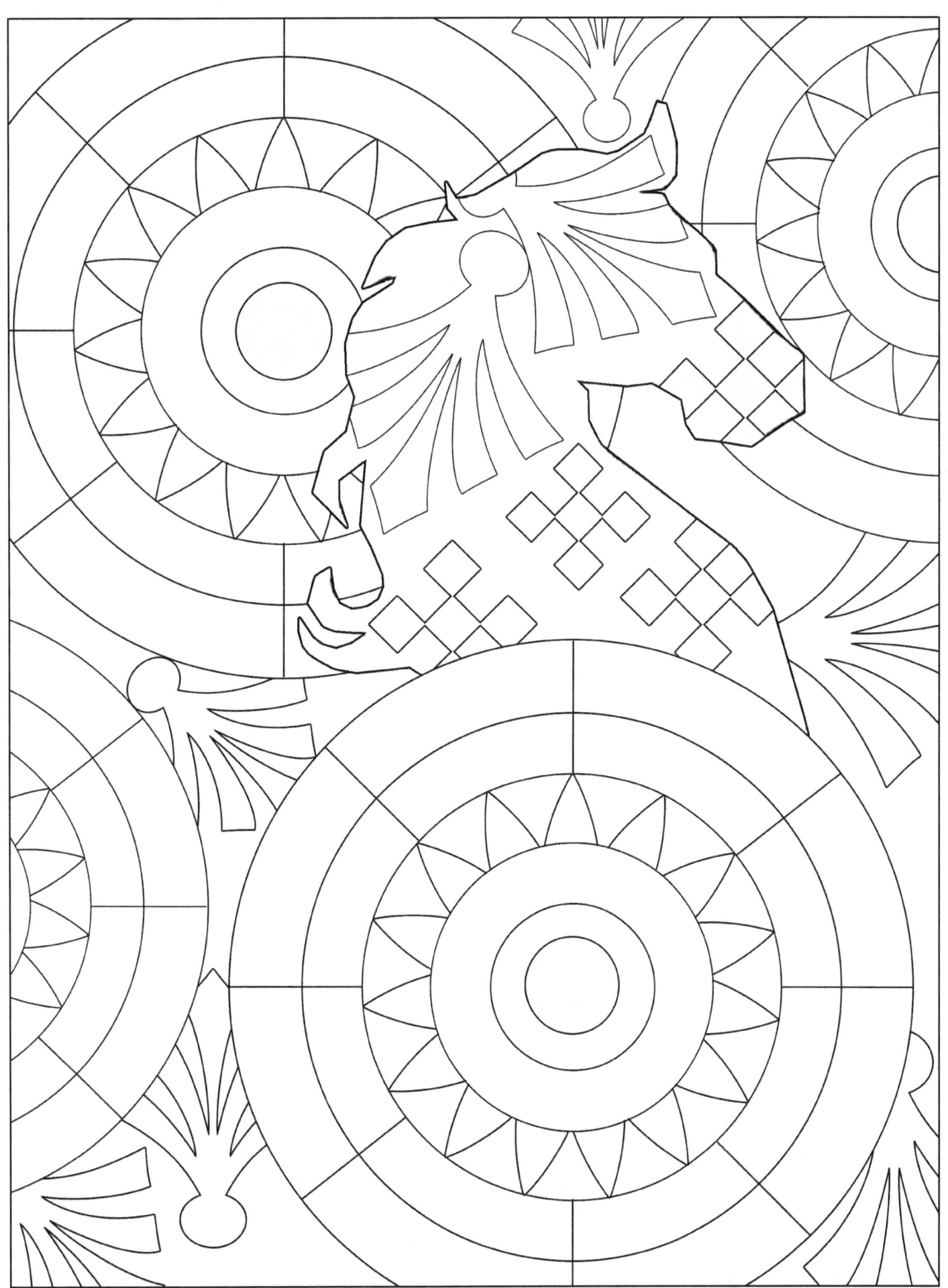

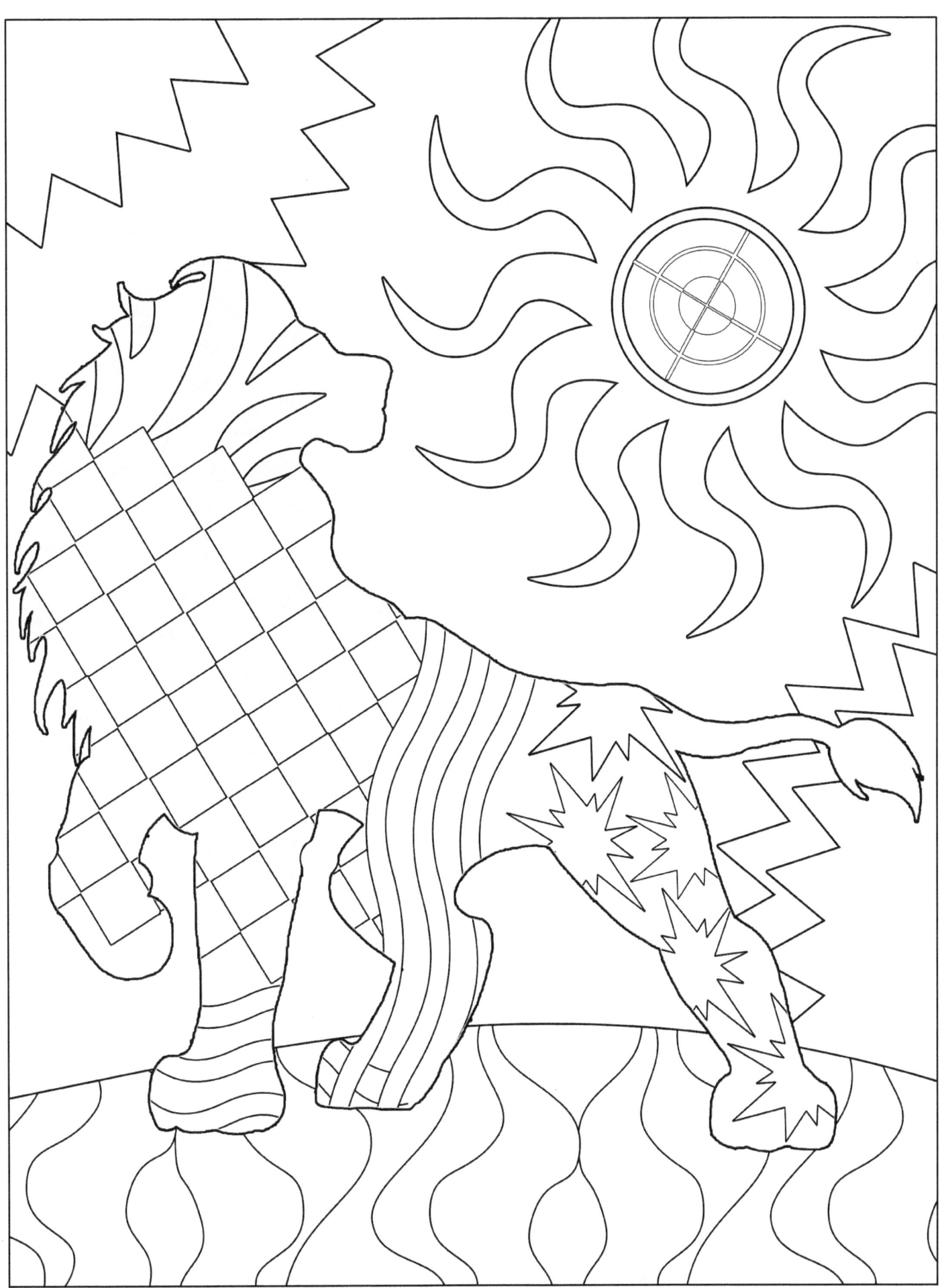

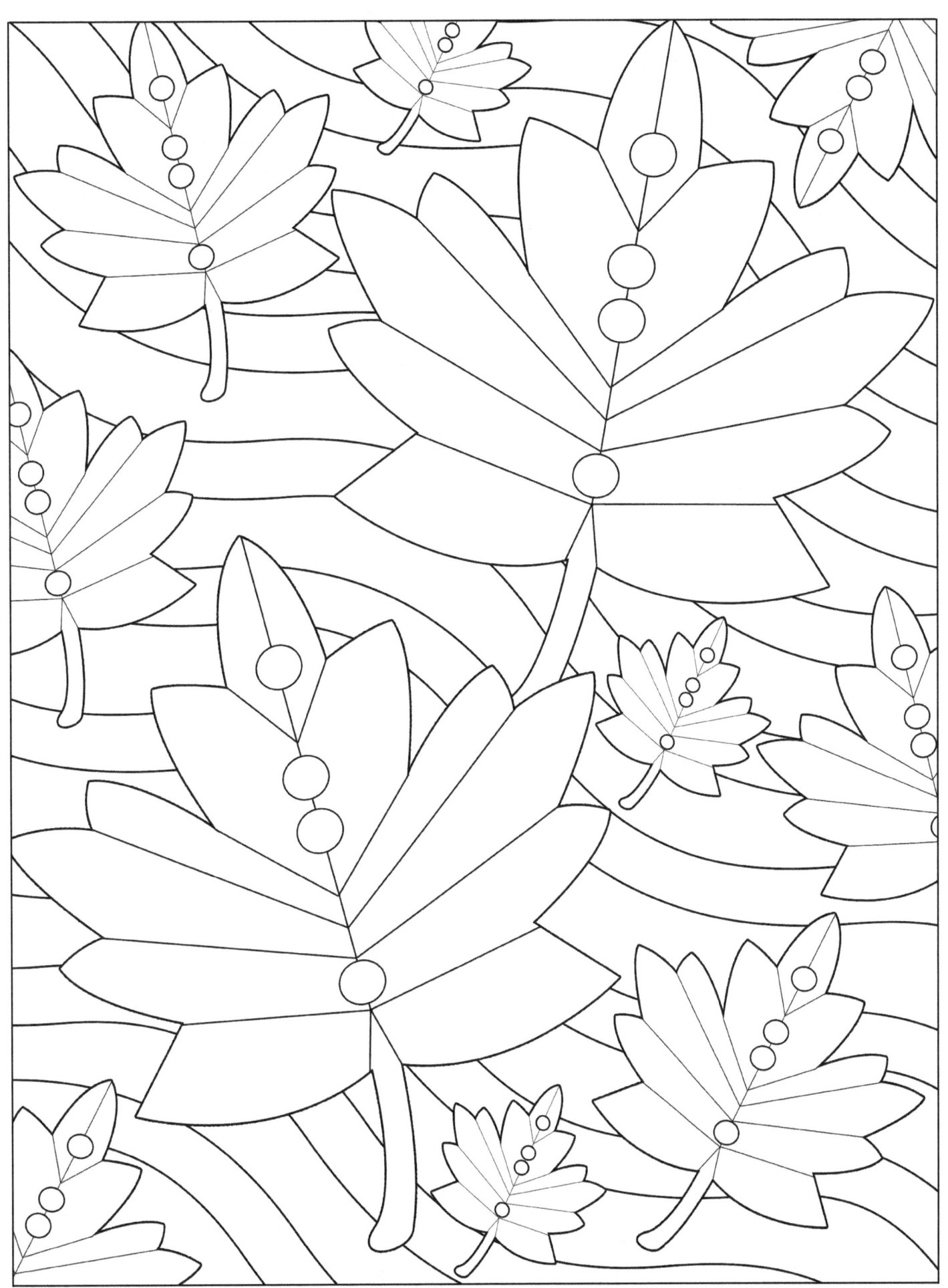

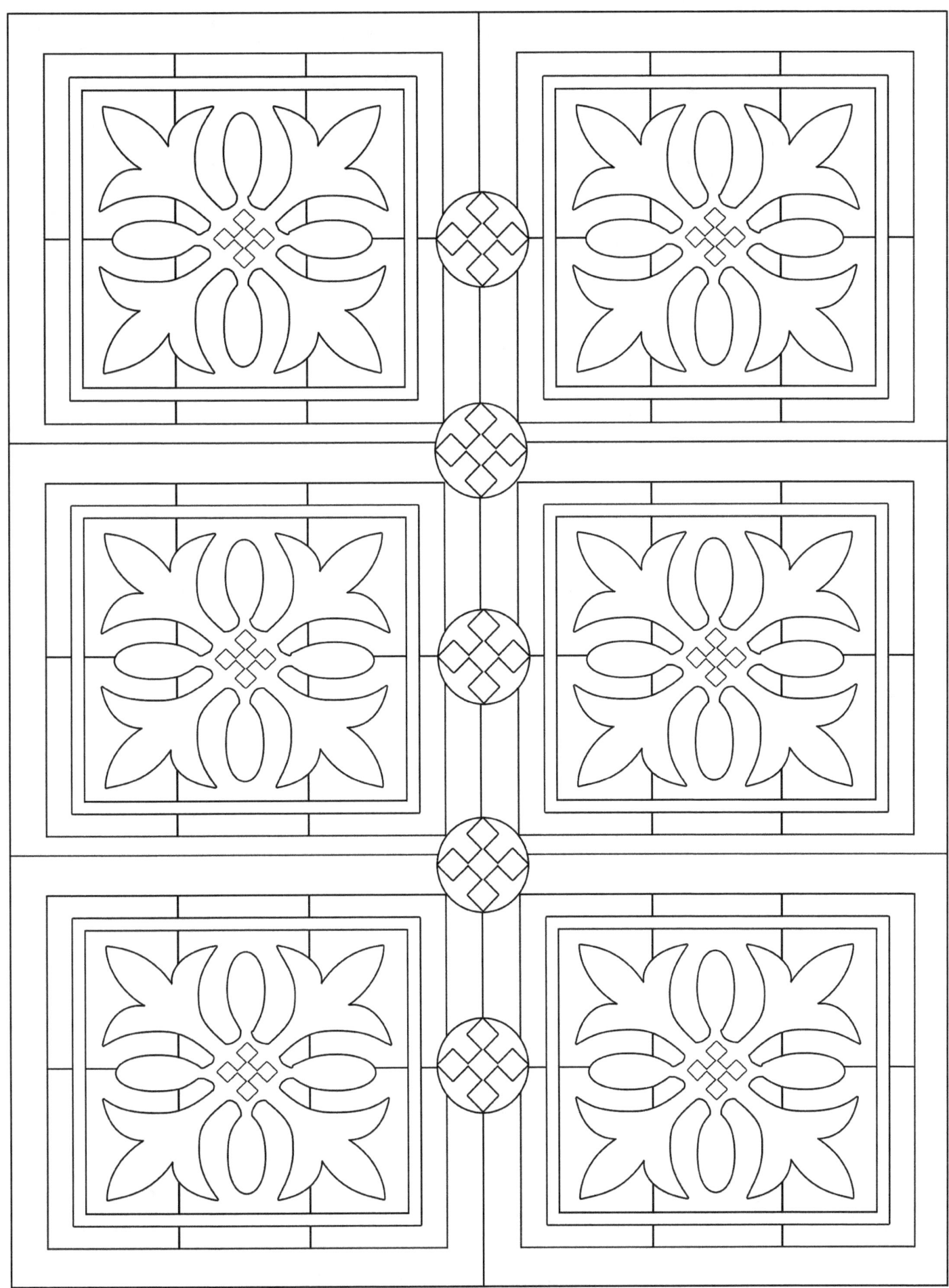

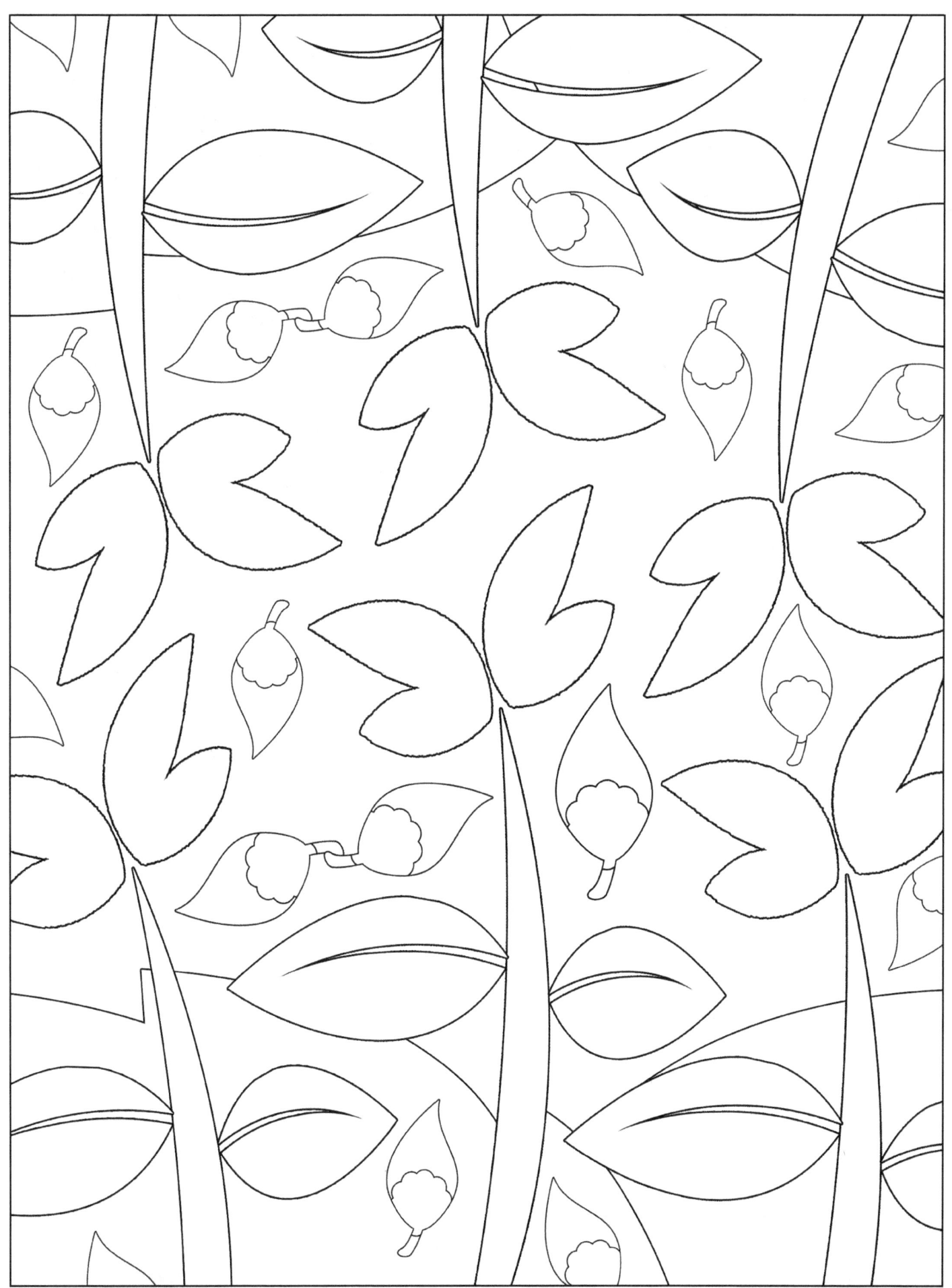

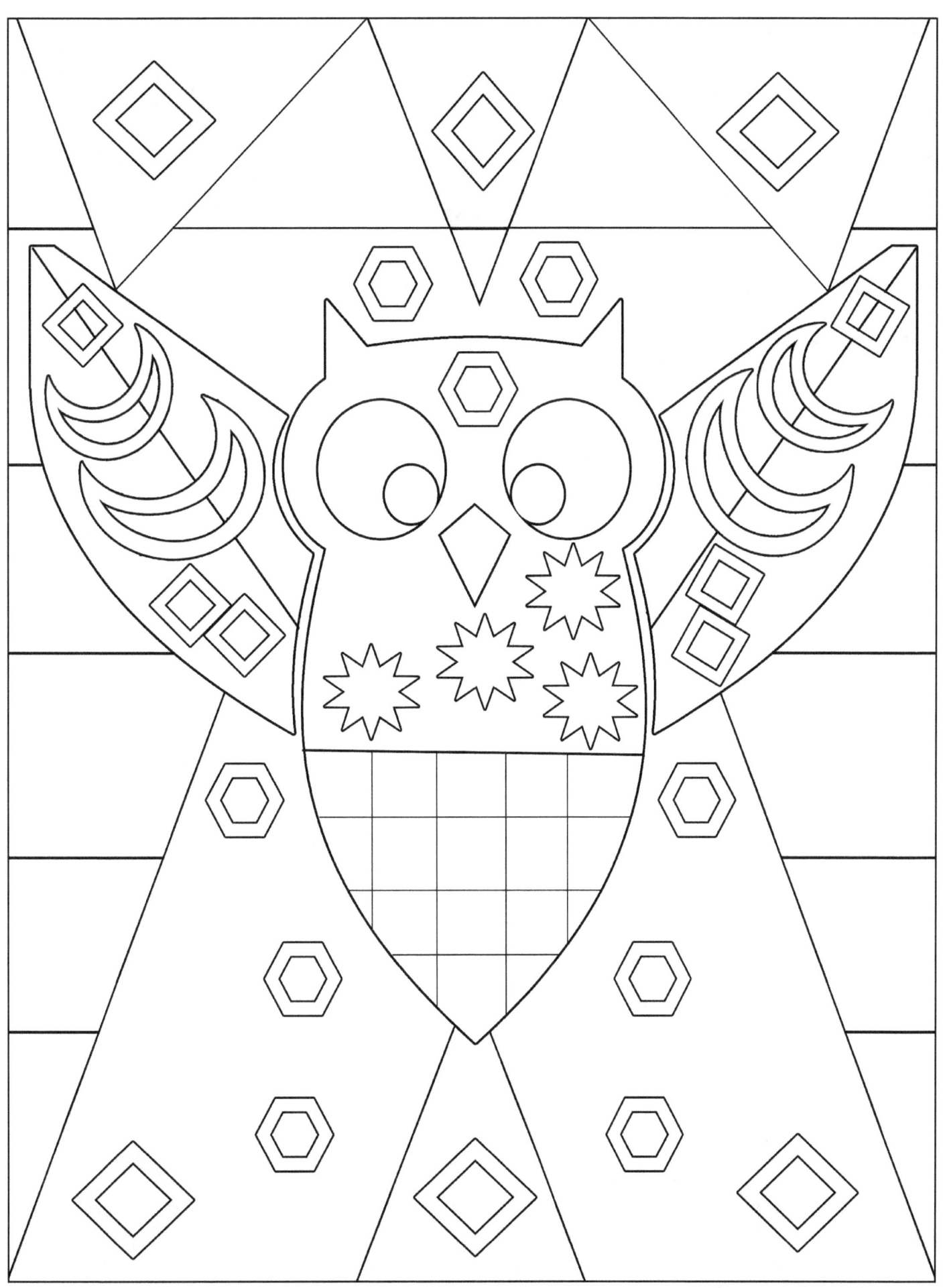

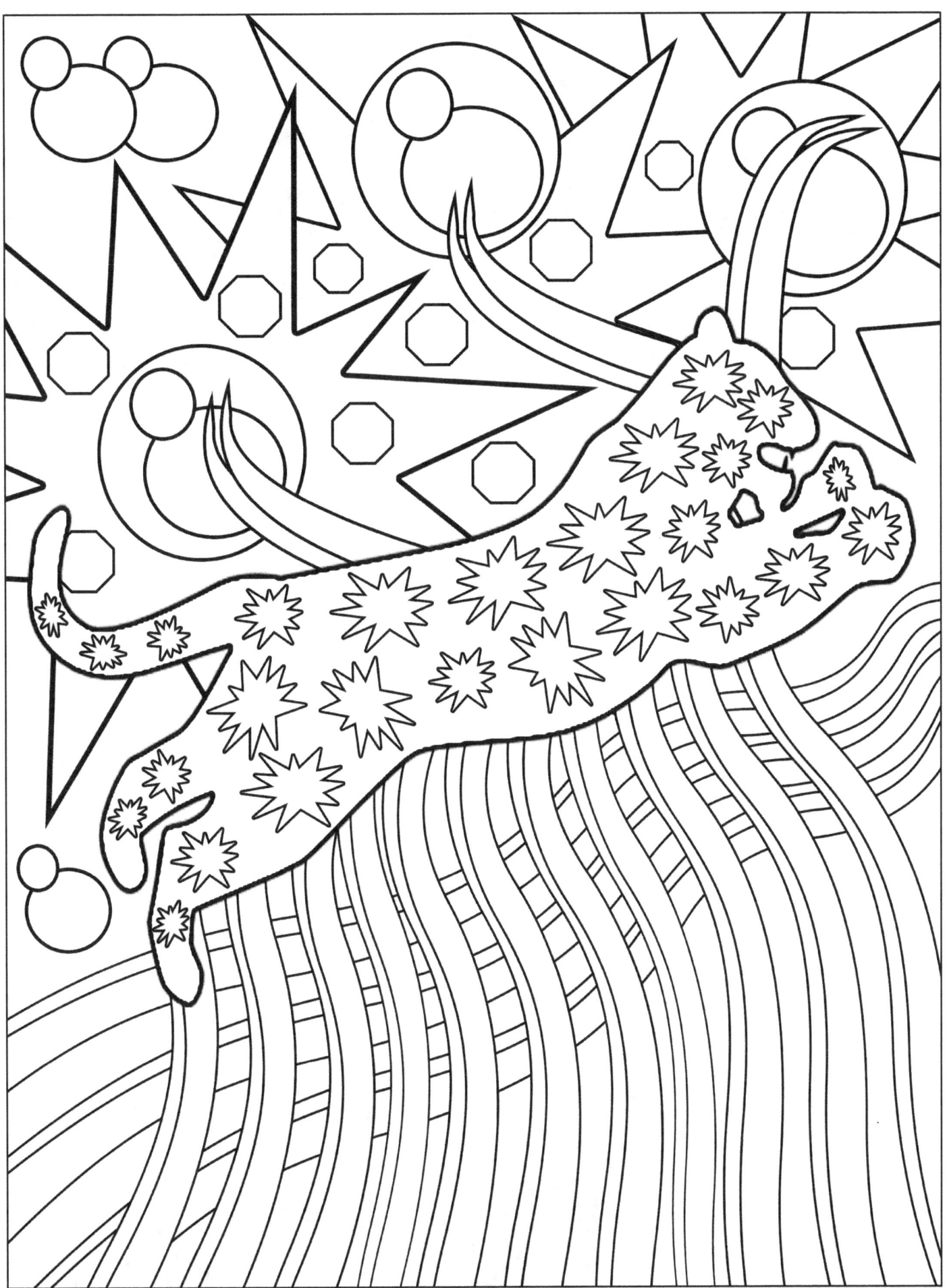

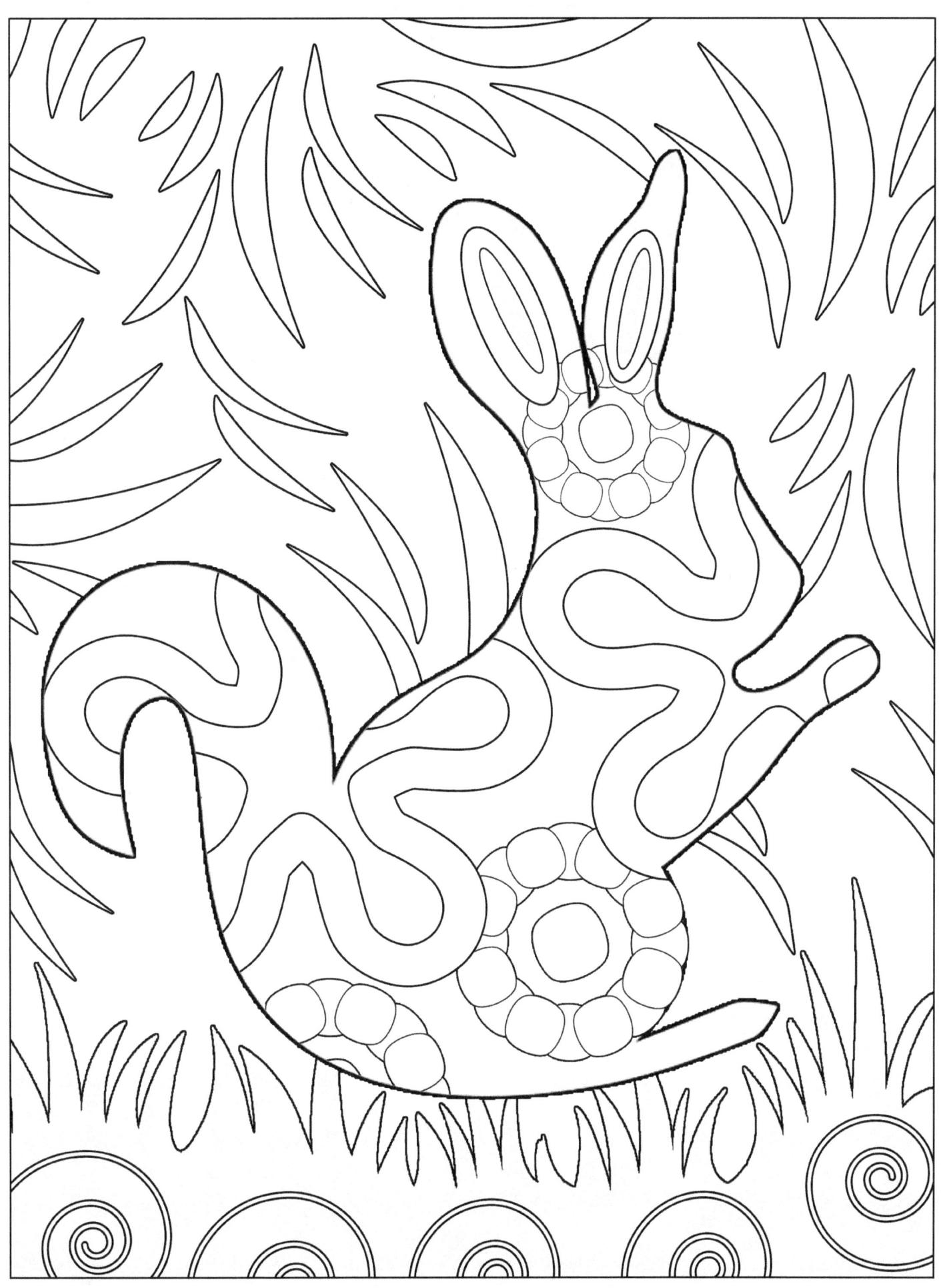

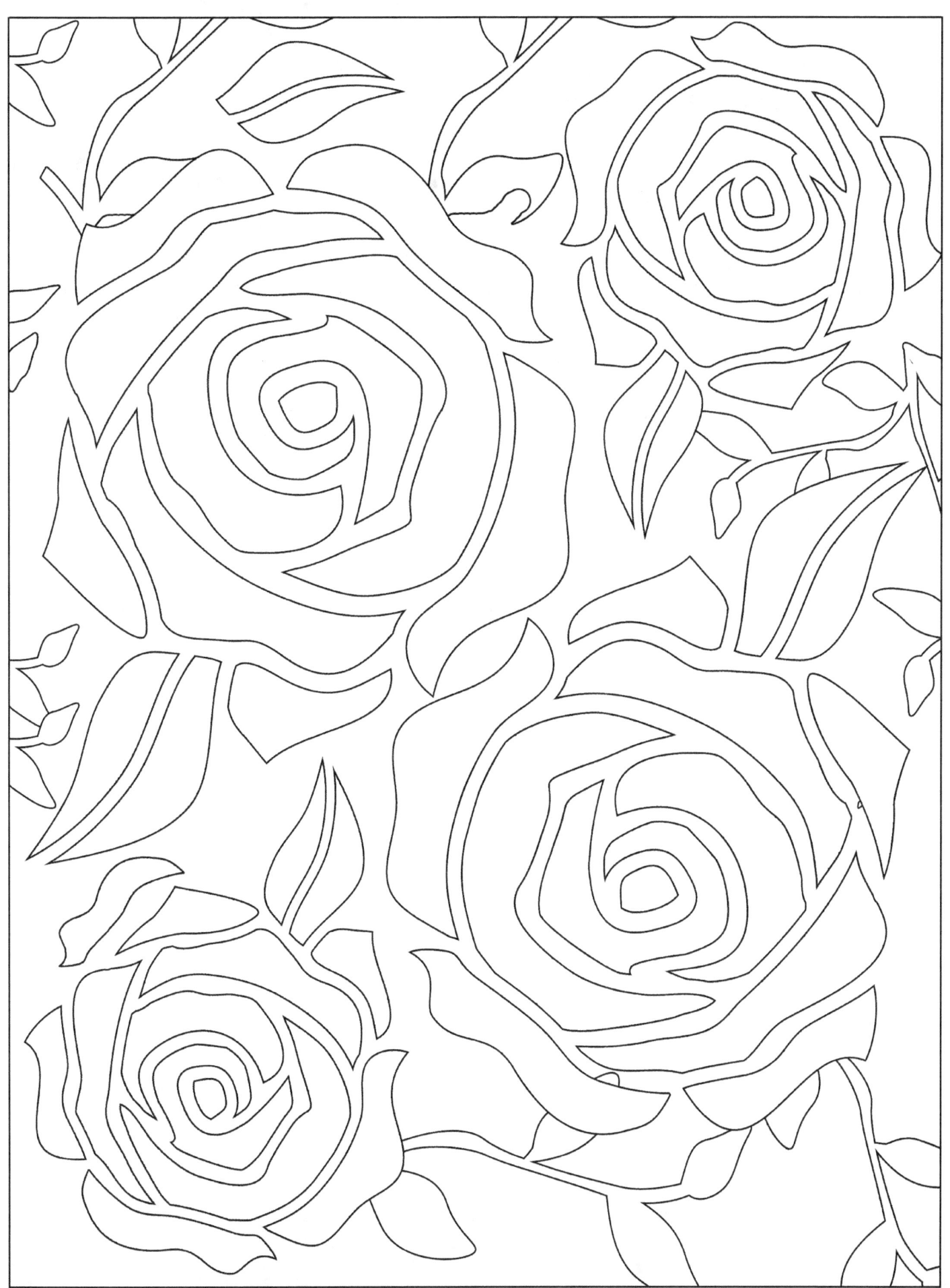

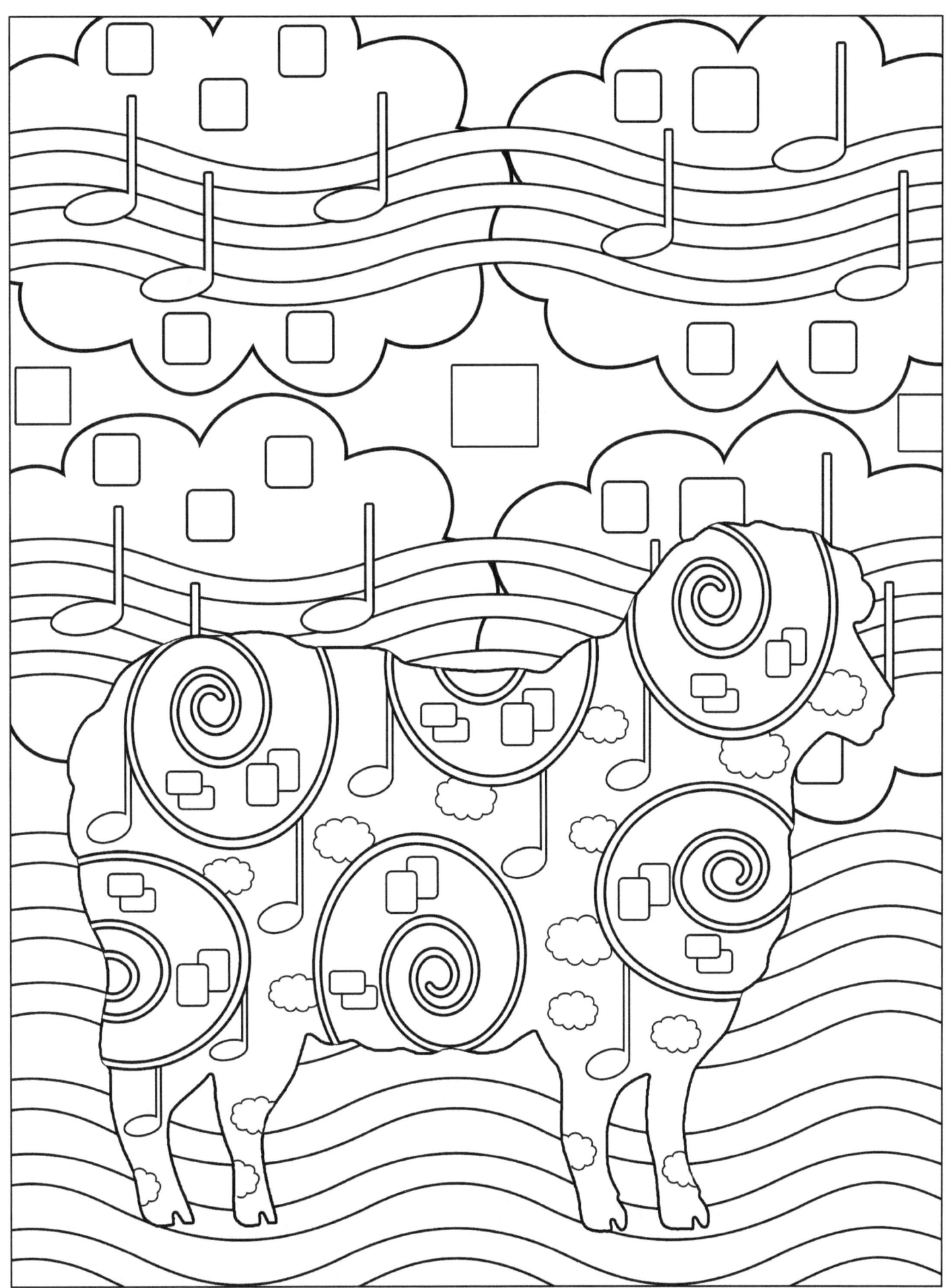

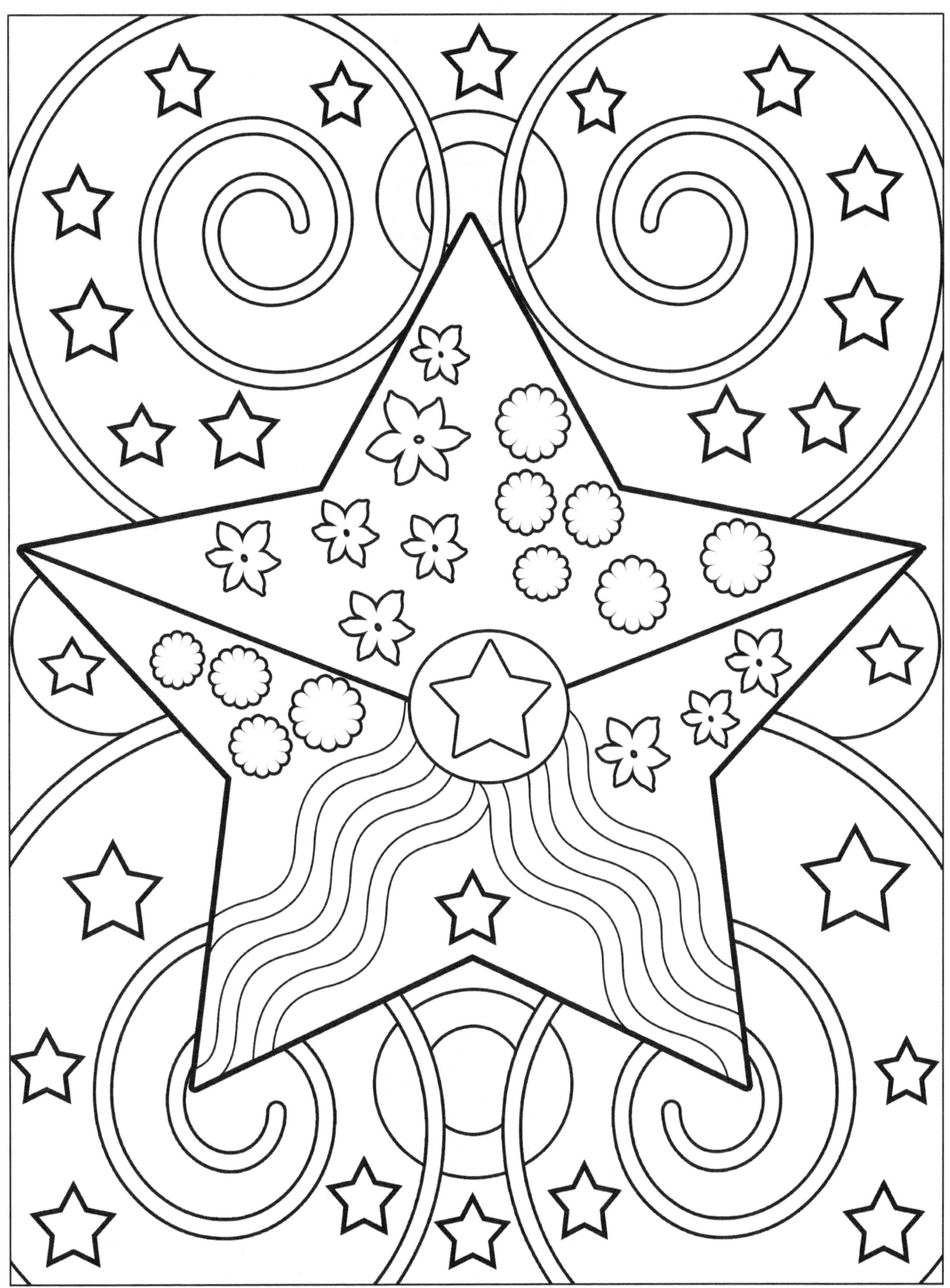

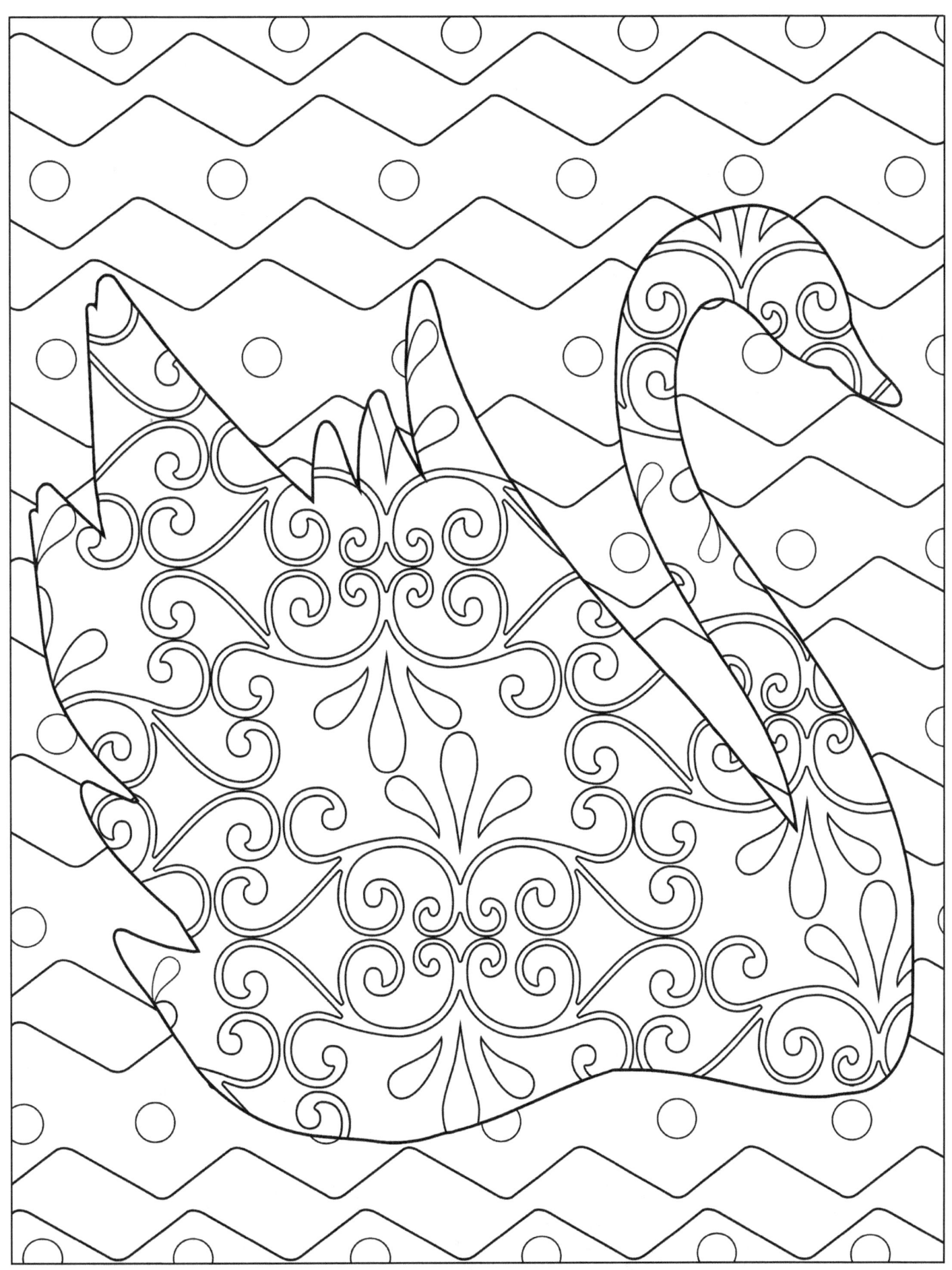

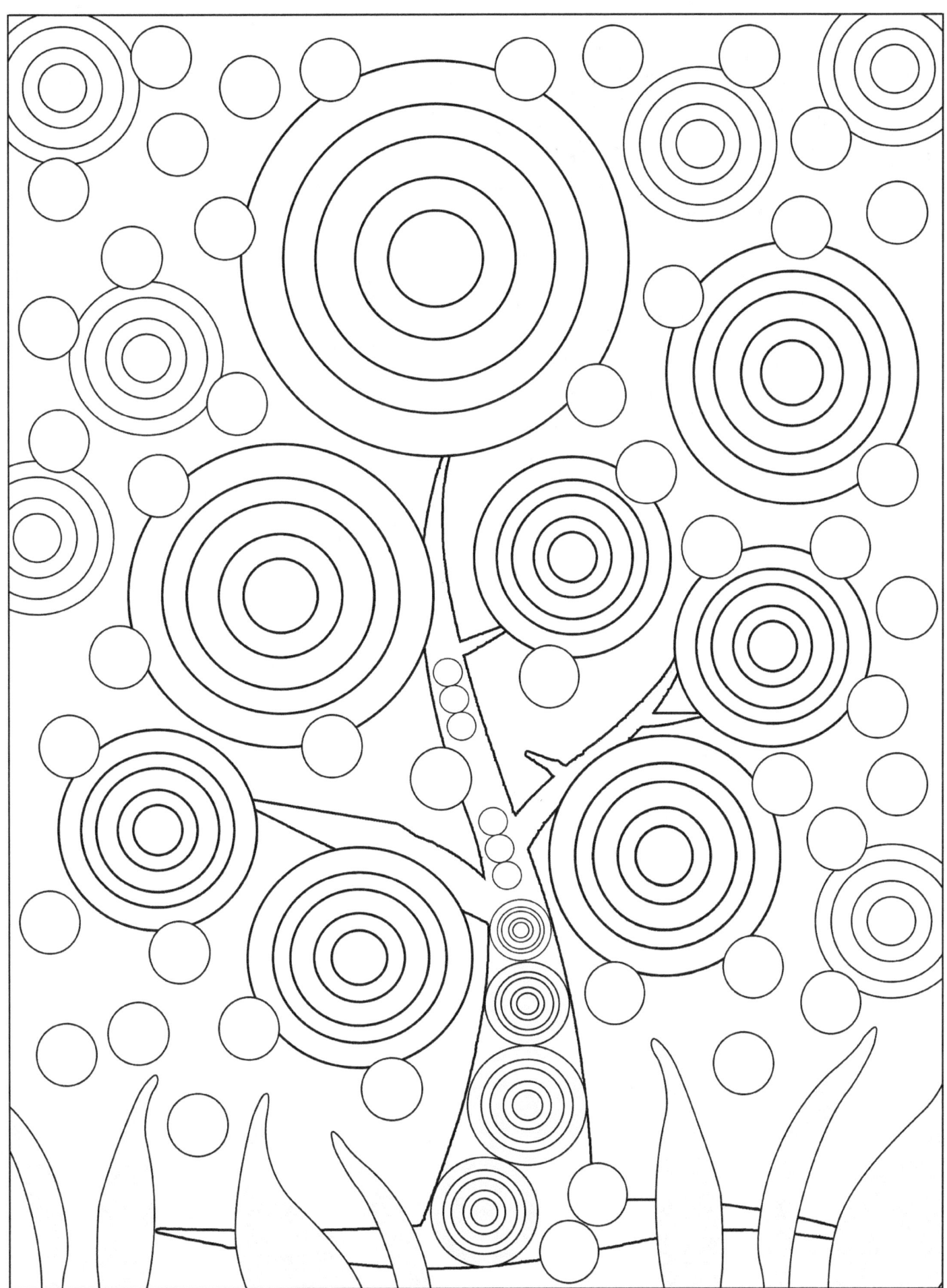

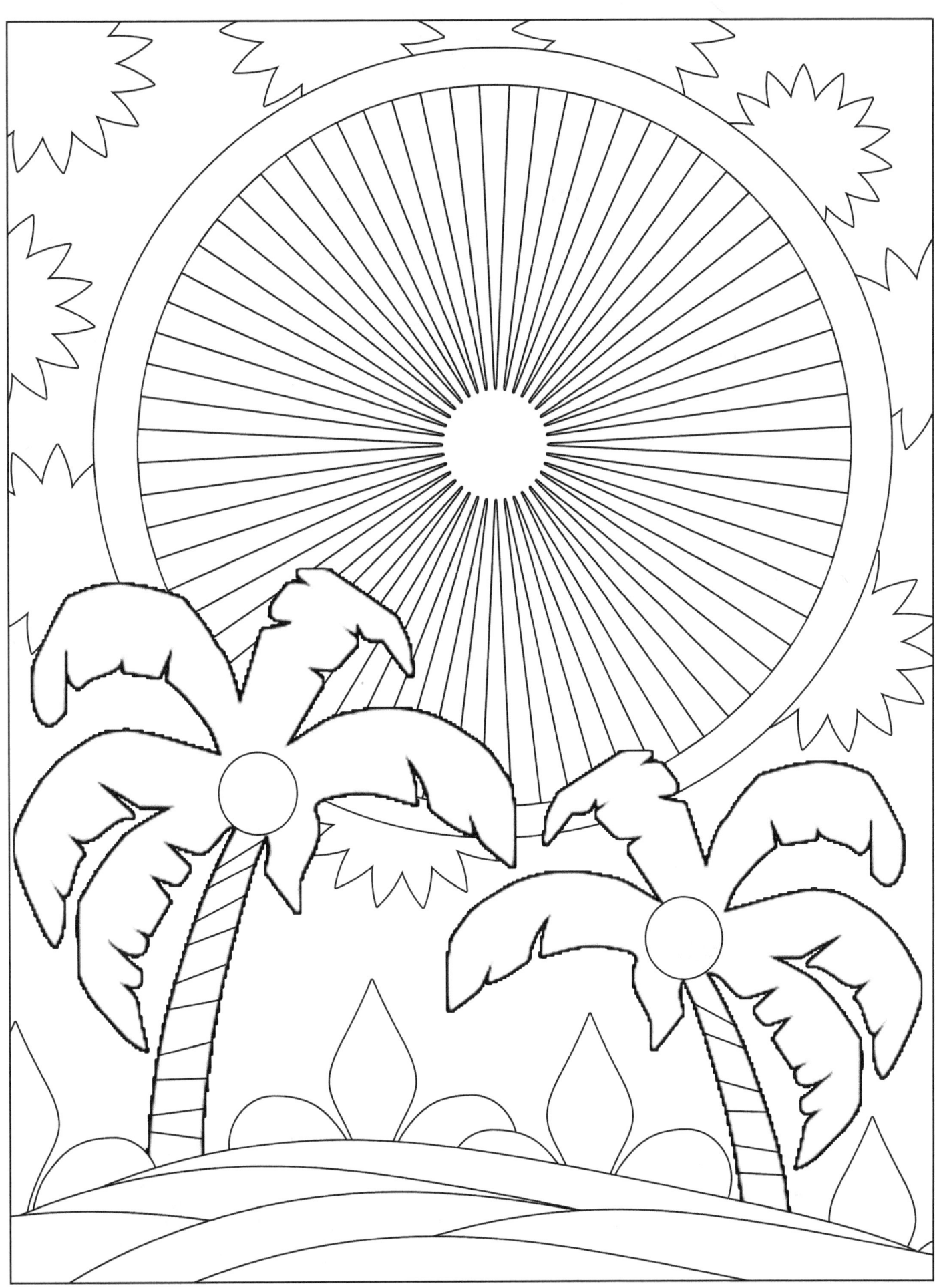

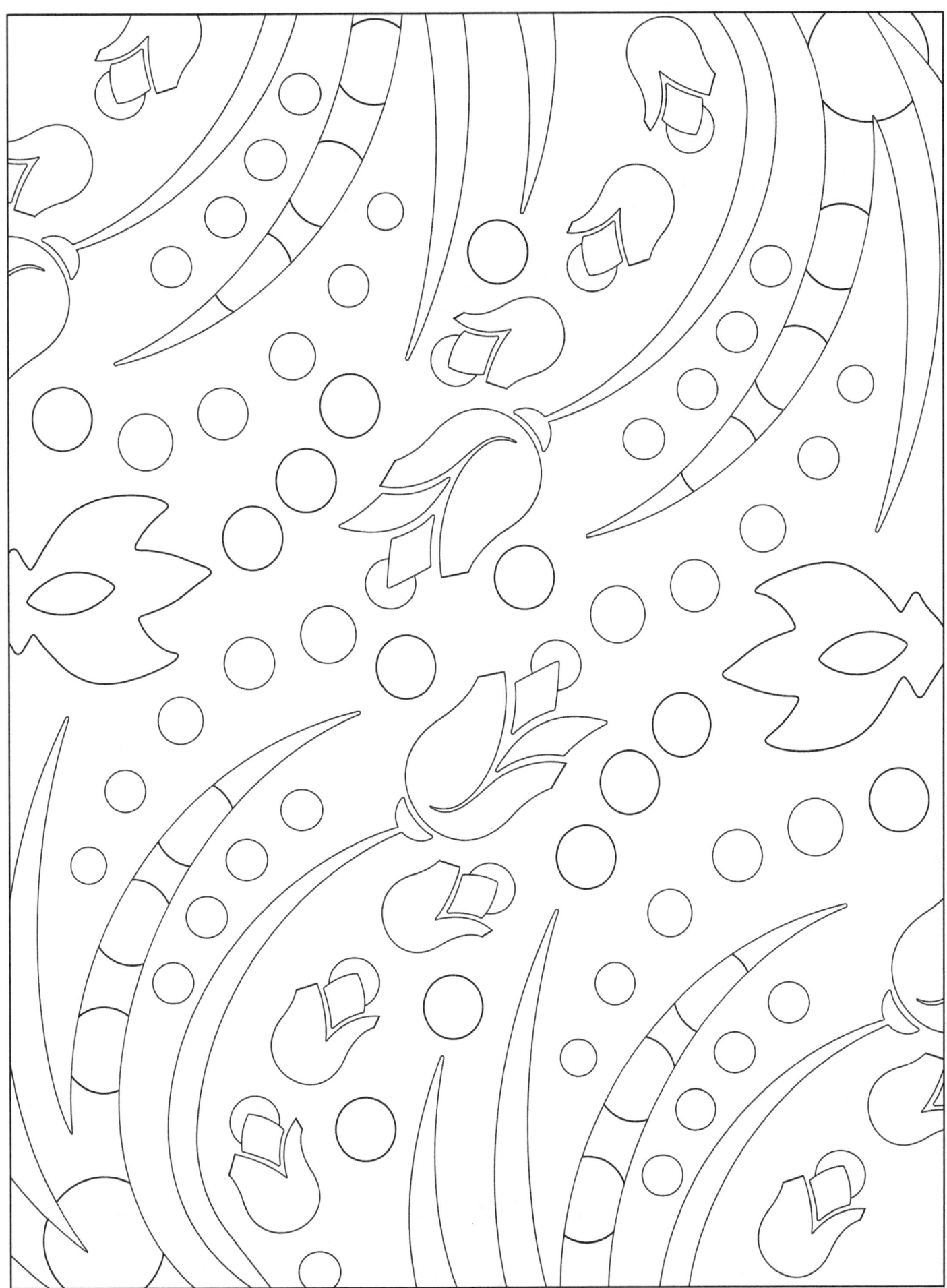

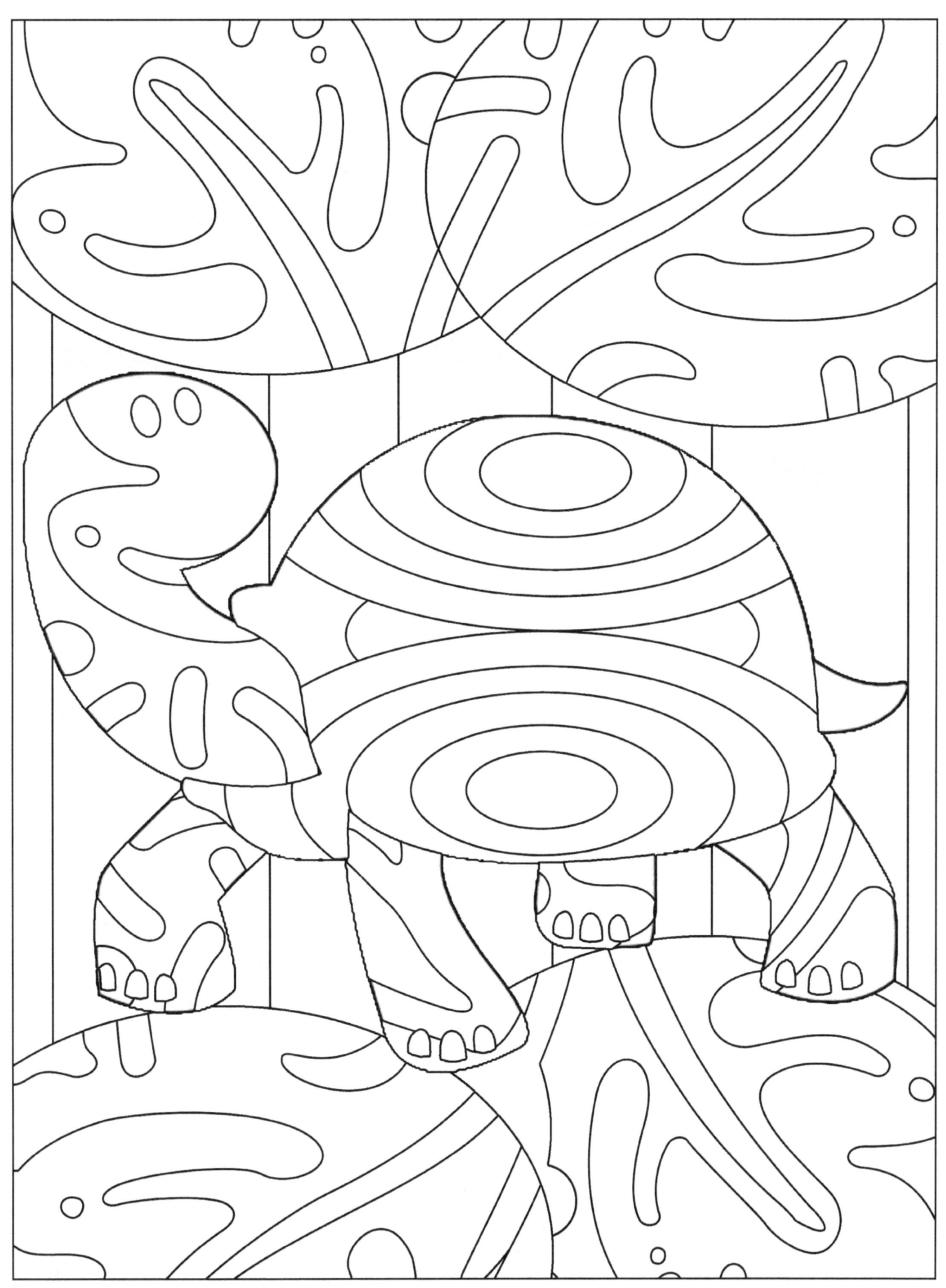

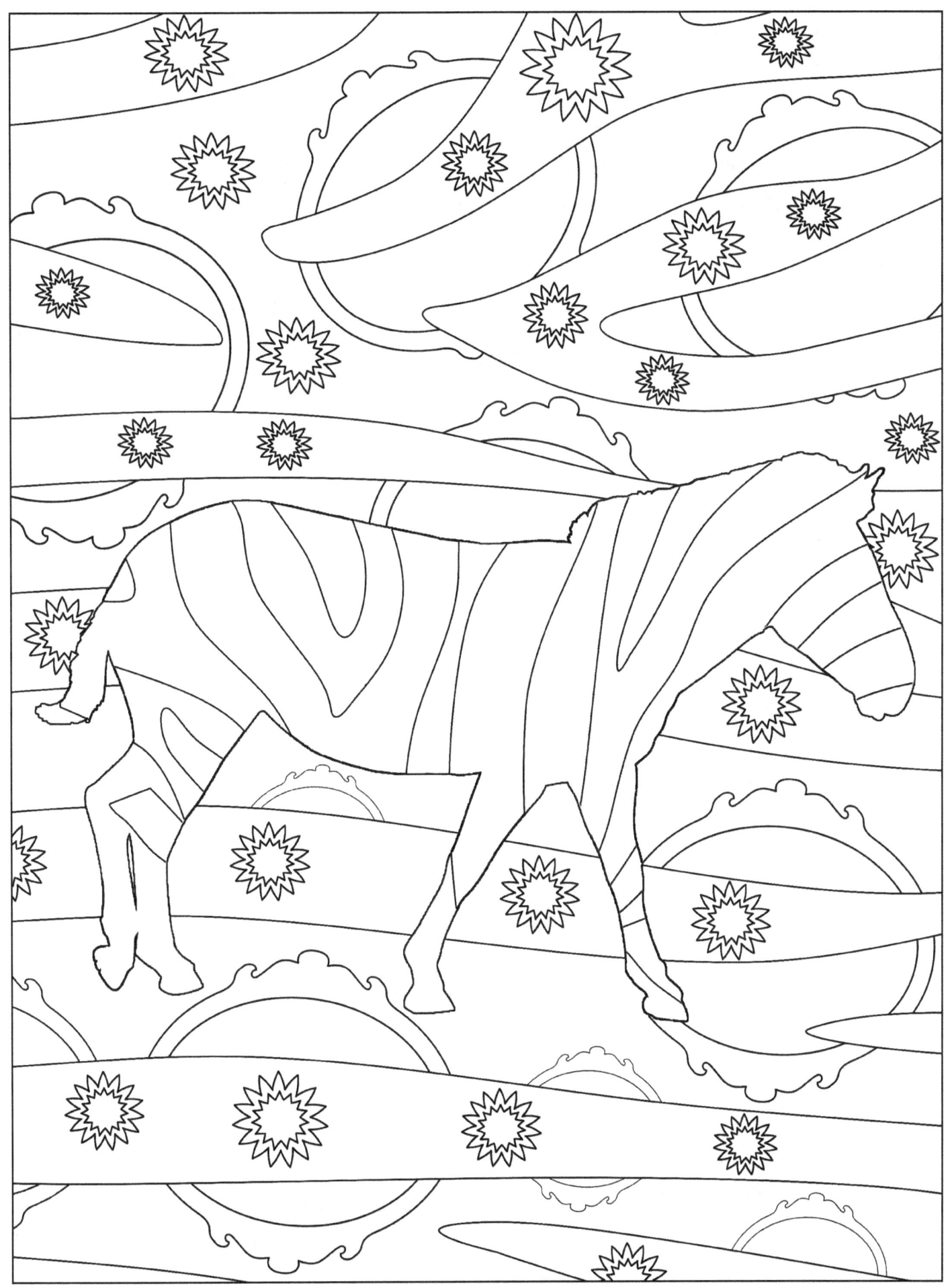

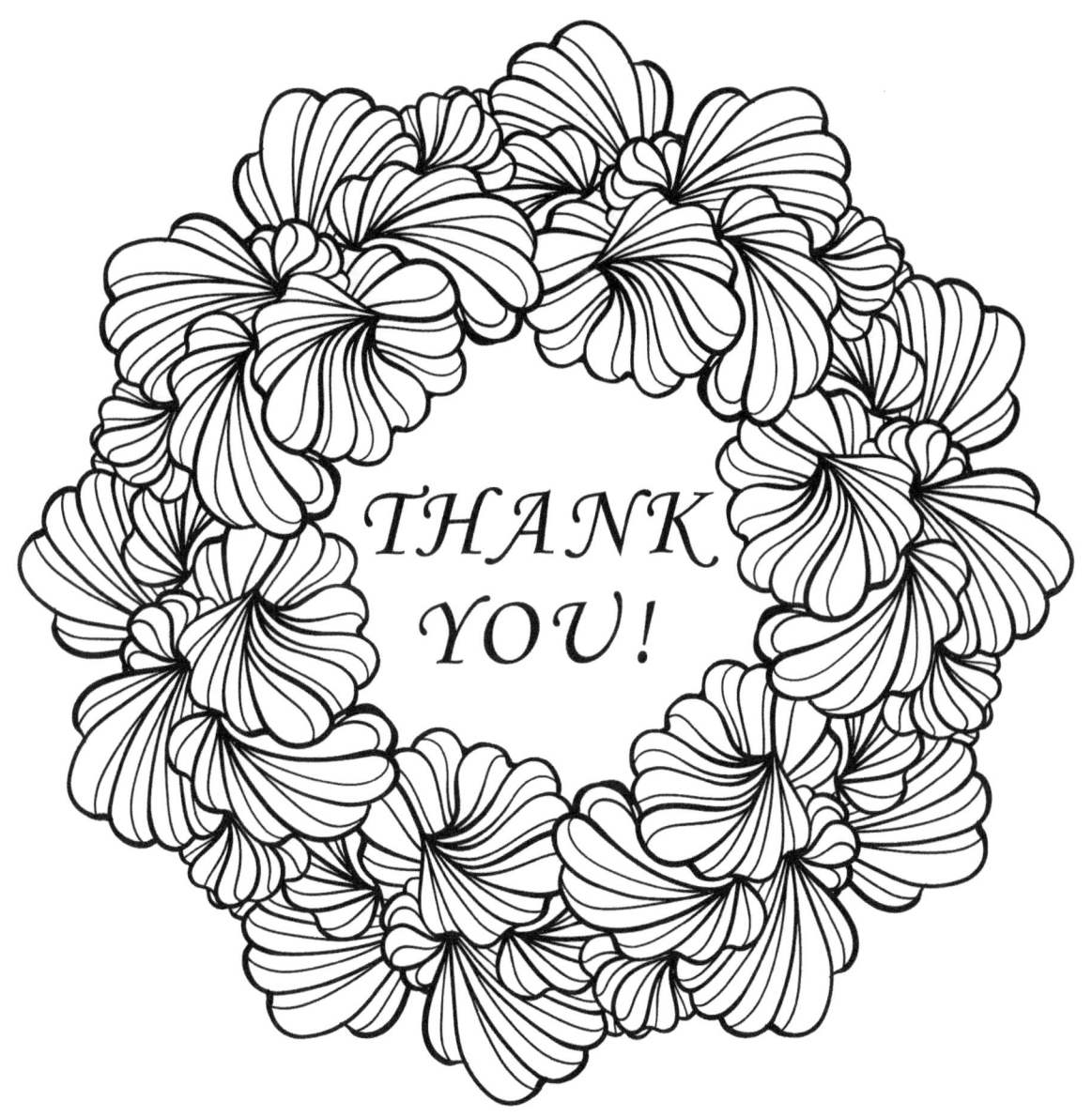

FROM THE AUTHOR

Thanks for coloring our book! I hope it was relaxing and I hope you had a lot of fun with it.

I would like to ask you for a *small* favor. Book reviews are very important for other coloring enthusiasts like you.

If you have a minute, please leave a comment under our book here: www.coloringcraze.com/**review2**

It will help the buyers to make a decision and your feedback will be priceless to our illustrators ☺

All our other books are available here: www.coloringcraze.com/**our-books**

Remember to grab your **Free Bonus!**

=> http://www.coloringcraze.com/**bonus** <=

Thank You!

www.ingramcontent.com/pod-product-compliance
Lightning Source LLC
Chambersburg PA
CBHW080831180526

45168CB00006B/2644

* 9 7 8 1 5 1 7 0 4 9 4 8 5 *